PROMOTION EXAMINATION PART 'D' 2014

These Notes have been prepared from the following prescribed and recommended books:

- S.N. Prasad, *The India-Pakistan War of 1965*
- Missed Opportunities: Indo-Pak War 1965, *Maj Gen Lachhman Singh*
- The Pakistan Army War 1965, *Maj Gen Shaukat Riza*
- In the Line of Duty: A Soldier Remembers, *Lt Gen Harbaksh Singh*

PENTAGON'S NOTES ON MILITARY HISTORY

PROMOTION EXAMINATION PART 'D' 2014

Col Harjeet Singh (Retd)

PENTAGON PRESS

Notes on Military History: Promotion Examination Part 'D'

Col Harjeet Singh (Retd)

ISBN 978-81-8274-721-0

First Published in 2013

Published by

PENTAGON PRESS
206, Peacock Lane
Shahpur Jat, New Delhi-110049
Phones: 011-64706243, 26491568
Telefax: 011-26490600
email: rajan@pentagonpress.in
website: www.pentagonpress.in

These Notes have been prepared from the following prescribed and recommended books:

- S.N. Prasad, *The India-Pakistan War of 1965*
- Missed Opportunities: Indo-Pak War 1965, *Maj Gen Lachhman Singh*
- The Pakistan Army War 1965, *Maj Gen Shaukat Riza*
- In the Line of Duty: A Soldier Remembers, *Lt Gen Harbaksh Singh*

Printed at Guide Offset Printers, New Delhi.

CONTENTS

LIST OF MAPS/SKETCHES

The 1965 War with Pakistan

BACKGROUND

The 1947-48 War between India and Pakistan concluded on 31 December 1948 and a ceasefire between the two warring nations came into existence on the mid-night of 31 December 1948/ 1 January 1949 under the auspices of the United Nations. Consequent to this, all hostilities came into an end, at the time. As a result of a Conference held between the two sides at Karachi (Pakistan), a formal Ceasefire Agreement was reached on 27 July 1949. In accordance with this Agreement, a ceasefire line was delineated, starting from a Point near Burejal, South West of Chhamb (East of this Point, the International Border was accepted as the Border between India and Pakistan.), running across numerous hills and valleys towards the West, and North to Keran, then East to Khor NJ 9842, and thence North to the Glaciers. Generally, the Line took into consideration the areas physically in possession of either side. A United Nations Military Observer Group for India and Pakistan (UNMOGIP), comprising officers from different countries was set up to supervise the truce.

It may be recalled that, when Pakistan invaded Kashmir, it was India that referred the matter to the United Nations. India complained of aggression, demanded that Pakistan be condemned, that forces under its control be expelled and that subsequently the wishes of the people could be ascertained. On the other hand, Pakistan contended that, in her opinion, Kashmir should have gone to Pakistan owing to religious affinity, that Indian forces should be withdrawn and that a plebiscite be held to determine the will of the people. The debates at the United Nations, unfortunately, were influenced by political bias and pressures; and a fair and objective view of the problem was not taken. Thus, in the crucial 13 August 1948 Resolution, while aggression was not condemned as such despite clear evidence presented by India, the United Nations resolved that Pakistan should withdraw her forces from Jammu and Kashmir and that the question of accession would be finally decided through a plebiscite. This amounted to indirect acceptance of the Pakistani aggression. Further a five-member United Nations Commission for India and Pakistan (UNCIP), in its resolution of 5 January 1949, had resolved that a ceasefire would be enforced, that the Pakistani forces would be withdrawn and India would be allowed to retain sufficient forces for the security of Kashmir, and that then only a plebiscite would be held under United Nations supervision. It may also be mentioned that Sir Owen Dixon, the United Nations negotiator mentioned in his final Report of 15 September 1950 that "when the frontier of the State of Jammu and Kashmir was crossed on, I believe, 20 October 1947, by hostile elements, it was contrary to International Law, and when in May 1948, as I believe, units of the regular Pakistan forces moved into the territory of the State, that too was inconsistent with International Law".

The cease fire stabilised, with about 12,950 square kilometres of area and seven hundred thousand inhabitants on the Pakistan side and about 209,790 square kilometres of area and three and half million people on the Indian side. However, Pakistan failed to withdraw the forces under her control, thus violating the United Nations resolution. As this was a pre-requisite to the holding of a plebiscite, the final part of the United Nations resolution, namely, the holding of a plebiscite could never be implemented. An impasse thus developed and continued. Ultimately, Dr. Frank Graham, the then United Nations mediator, recommended a settlement through direct Indo-Pakistan negotiations, in 1953.

At this stage, it would be worth mentioning the developments within Jammu and Kashmir itself. In pursuance of the Instrument of Accession, India took several measures to give the people of Jammu and Kashmir a democratic set-up and maximum possible autonomy, which no other State enjoyed. Article 370 had been introduced in the India Constitution (adopted on 26 November 1949) which gives a special status to Jammu and Kashmir and ensures the protection of the identity of the people and promotion of their interests. This article limited the powers of the Indian Parliament to make laws about certain matters included in the Union list and the Concurrent list; whereby considerable autonomy was permitted to the State, as opposed to the other States of the Indian Union. Further, although this article was inserted as a temporary provision, it could only be done away with on the recommendation of the Constituent Assembly of the State. By including this special provision, the identity and interests of the Kashmiris was fully taken care of. The whole idea of the Founding Fathers of Free India was to fully take care of any apprehensions of the Kashmiris at large regarding their identity and to bring about emotional integration with the rest of the country in course of time. Elections were held to a Constituent Assembly for the State and a Constituent Assembly was established in October 1951. This Assembly fully ratified the accession of the State to India, on 6 February 1954. Further, this Assembly drew up a separate Constitution for the State, as envisaged in Article 370 of the Indian Constitution and this was adopted subsequently on 17 November 1956.

This Constitution also re-affirmed the State's accession to India. Section 3 of the Constitution says, "The State of Jammu and Kashmir is and shall be an integral part of the Union of India," Section 4 of the Constitution says, "The territory of the State shall comprise all the territories which on the Fifteenth day of August, 1947, were under the sovereignty or suzerainty of the Ruler of the State", (i.e., including the Pakistan Occupied Area of Jammu and Kashmir). Section 13 of the Constitution says, "The prime object of the State consistent with the ideals and objectives of the freedom movement envisaged in "New Kashmir" shall be the promotion of the welfare of the mass of the people by establishing and preserving a socialist order of society wherein all exploitation of man has been abolished and wherein justice—social, economic and political—shall inform all the institutions of national life." Section 25 of the Constitution says, "The State shall combat ignorance, superstition, fanaticism, communalism, racialism, cultural backwardness and shall seek to foster brotherhood and equality, among all communities under the aegis of a Secular State." Section 48 of the Constitution reserves 24, out of the 100 Assembly seats, for people of the area under Pakistani occupation. Section 147 prohibits any amendments to Section 3, i.e., the relationship of the State with the Union of India. It may be mentioned that the State has, ever since, been functioning under this Special Constitution. Thus, accession of Jammu and Kashmir to India was legal, completely constitutional and irrevocable. Elections have been held at regular intervals, people have been fully participating in these, and elected Governments of their choice. Successive State Governments, led by their duly elected leaders including Sheikh Mohammed Abdullah, have all along been reiterating that the accession of the State to India was irrevocable and that there was no question of reopening the issue. The question of a plebiscite does not arise either.

In the early years of its rule, the National Conference Government not only gave a Constitution to the State, based on the party's promise to develop a 'Naya Kashmir' (New Kashmir), based on Socialistic, Secular, Democratic Principles, but also created a National Militia, took effective measures for the spread of literacy, brought about land reforms whereby land was distributed to the tenants, some industries were set up, economic condition of the people was improved and cultural activities were given a boost. By and large, the people could feel the benefits of the change from an autocratic Government to a democratic Government However, there were some elements in the State, particularly fundamentalistic and theocratic (though small in number), who opposed the accession.

Equally, there were also radical elements among the Hindus, who opposed any special dispensation for the Kashmiris, such as Article 370. The National Conference Government was somewhat harsh in its treatment of all these elements, who were opposed to them and thus alienated them to some extent. By 1952, reforms introduced to give the majority Muslim population in the Valley their legitimate dues which they were denied earlier, resulted in resentment among the Hindu population, particularly of Jammu area, which could not forget the earlier supremacy that they exercised in the State. Agitations were resorted to and the Government used strong methods to deal with them. Owing to pressures brought about on them, the Central Government had to intervene; and this caused resentment not only among a section of the Muslim population of the Valley but also in some elements of the National Conference Government led by Sheikh Abdullah. During this period, an Agreement, which came to be known as the Delhi Agreement, was reached between the Government of India and the Government of Jammu and Kashmir on 24 July 1952, which brought about some changes in the Constitutional relationship of the State with India, whereby democracy and economic development were to get further momentum in the State. However, the pro-Pakistani elements agitated against the introduction of such reforms. Sheikh Abdullah got pressurised to take a negative attitude and went back on the Delhi Agreement. The Central Government, in turn, dismissed and arrested him on 8 August 1953.

The arrest of Sheikh Abdullah led to significant changes in the political climate of Jammu and Kashmir. Bakshi Ghulam Mohammed took over leadership in the State and put down the pro-Pakistani elements firmly. Some of the National Conference leaders broke away from the Party. Ghulam Mohiuddin Kara started a new Party known as the Political Conference in June 1953. Mirza Afzal Beg started another party known as the Plebiscite Front. Bakshi made it clear that accession of the State was complete and that there was no question of a plebiscite. He also stated that the only problem pending was the liberation of the portion of the State which was in adverse occupation of Pakistan. The Delhi Agreement was ratified by the State Constituent Assembly on 6 February 1954. General Elections to the State Legislature were held in 1957 and 1962 and the people fully participated in these; and elected governments of their choice.

On 22 February 1954, a Military Agreement between United States and Pakistan was announced, whereby large quantities of sophisticated American weapons were to be supplied to Pakistan, ostensibly to resist the so-called Communist threat. India protested vehemently, making clear her apprehensions that the aid would really be used against India and that the Cold War between the two Super Powers was being forced into the Sub-Continent. Subsequent events left little doubt in anybody's mind, as was evident from the manner in which Pakistan used her American-acquired equipment against India. This had happened despite assurances by the Pakistani Prime Minister Mohammed Ali in writing to Nehru that American arms would not be used against India, and despite assurances by the then American President that America would frustrate any efforts by Pakistan to violate the Agreement. A message from President Eisenhower to Nehru dated 24 February 1954 said,

> ...and I am confirming publicly, that if our aid to any country, including Pakistan, is misused and directed against another in aggression, I will undertake immediately, in accordance with my constitutional authority, appropriate action both within and without the United Nations to thwart such aggression."

It may be recalled that at the time the Military Agreement was concluded, the only Communist threat to Pakistan could have been from China (the relations between the Soviet Union and China were cordial at the time), but the terrain and the conditions on the Northern border were such that China was not in a position to pose even a minor military threat to Pakistan. There is a school of thought that considers that Pakistan was apprehensive that India controlled its vital river waters, most of which flowed through Kashmir, and as such needed to strengthen herself to deal with India. However, despite the satisfactory conclusion of the Indus Waters Agreement in 1960, Pakistan continued to build herself up. Utilisation of military aid thrice against India, subsequently, in order to settle territorial issues by force, leaves no doubt about Pakistan's intentions in concluding such military pacts.

In fact, by concluding the Military Agreement with the United States, and by subsequently joining military pacts such as Central Treaty Organisation (CENTO) and South East Asian Treaty Organisation (SEATO), Pakistan had literally brought the Cold War into the Indian Sub-continent. Naturally, India which was dedicated to a policy of Non-Alignment and Friendship with all nations, all along opposed any military pacts. Further, with her neighbour being heavily armed, India had to look to other quarters, including the Soviet Union, for buying her essential requirements of military hardware, for her own security. An idea can be had of the magnitude of the problem faced by India, from the fact that the United States aid amounted to 1.5 billion dollars at the time, and that this included over 200 M-45 Patton tanks, one Squadron M-104A Supersonic Fighters, four Squadrons F-86F Fighters and two Squadrons B-75B Bombers. None of this equipment could have been effectively used in the Northern border area of Pakistan, against any so-called Communist threat. This had completely upset the relative strength between India and Pakistan.

The United States had her own reasons for equipping Pakistan. She, along with other Western nations, was apprehensive of Communist expansion and evolved a defence line from Western Europe to Japan, more or less along the borders of the Communist countries to contain it. This line was to be manned by the countries along this border, who would take the first land thrust. These countries were to be backed by the armed might of the United States, both conventional and nuclear. With the development of the SEATO and CENTO, in addition to the North Atlantic Treaty Organisation (NATO), the Western Powers thus felt that the threat to the 'Free World' from the Communist Powers, particularly Soviet Union and China, was contained. Pakistan is one such country, which continues to figure in the Western strategic plans.

India had been accepting economic assistance for her development from various countries, including the United States and the Soviet Union. On the question of Kashmir, the Soviet Union progressively saw the correctness of the Indian stand and supported Indian in the United Nations. In 1956, the Soviet Union is reported to have even offered India military assistance but India had declined it, as it went against her well-known policies.

Taking advantage of subsequent Sino-Soviet differences and rupture of relations between China and India, Pakistan started wooing China from about 1955. Over a period of time, this had resulted in development of relations between the two countries to the extent that on 2 March 1963 a provisional Border Treaty between the two countries was announced whereby certain territory of Kashmir in the Northern area in adverse possession of Pakistan was ceded to China. In turn, Pakistan received support of China on the Kashmir issue.

As a result of the Chinese invasion of India in 1962, India having suffered some reverses was compelled by force of circumstances to accept military aid from the Western nations. Although the aid received was very limited in scope (mainly small arms) and could only be useful in mountain warfare, Pakistan protested vehemently towards the so-called Indian rearmament. This was in sharp contrast to the type of aid (tanks, APCs, guns and so on) provided to Pakistan, which could be utilised against India in the plains. Pakistan insisted that there was really no threat to India from China and that any aid to India should only be provided if India agreed to settle the Kashmir problem. Although the United States did not accept these conditions, the complete aid promised to India originally, was not delivered during this period. India also received some limited aid from the Soviet Union in order to meet any renewed Chinese attack. As usual, the Pakistanis protested against this also.

A further development as a result of the Chinese attack against India was that efforts to evolve a solution to the Kashmir issue were renewed, particularly by the Western Powers (USA and UK). During the negotiations Pakistan demanded division of Jammu and Kashmir whereby she would get about 220,150 square kilometres of territory including the Kashmir Valley, and a plebiscite to be held within six months pending which foreign troops be inducted and given control of the Valley. On the other hand, India was prepared to consider stabilisation generally on the basis of the Ceasefire Line, sign a No-War Pact with Pakistan and effect a disengagement of troops. Six separate meetings were held during 1962-63 but did not result in any agreement. An event of significance during this period was that, due to virulent anti-Indian propaganda against India and communal riots, about seven hundred thousand refugees crossed from Pakistan into India in 1964. This had naturally resulted in further deterioration of relations between the two countries.

Within Kashmir, under the Kamaraj Plan, Bakshi resigned in 1963 and Mir Shamsuddin took over the leadership. An incident then occurred that shook the entire Kashmir Valley. Prophet Mohammed's holy hair was found missing from the Hazratbal shrine in Srinagar on 7 December 1963. The Kashmiris were infuriated and particularly the Opposition parties got together and more or less paralysed the functioning of the Administration. Fortunately, the relic was retraced and securely lodged in the shrine. However, Shamsuddin had to make way for Ghulam Mohammed Sadiq in February 1964. Sadiq had the vision to realize that, for democracy and secularism to thrive in the State and for emotional integration of it with India, it was necessary to follow much more liberal policies. Accordingly, he took various measures including the release of Sheikh Abdullah. Considerable freedom was permitted, normalcy was restored and administration was improved all-round. However, in due course, both the pro-Pakistan elements as well as the Hindu reactionary elements took advantage of the liberal policy of Sadiq and pursued their objectives with renewed vigour. There was an effort to abrogate Article 370, but this was fiercely resisted. Although, the idea was given up, certain Articles, e.g., 356 and 357 of the Indian Constitution were extended to Jammu and Kashmir. Further, communal riots taking place in various parts of the country, accentuated the apprehensions of the people in the Valley. Shri Jai Prakash Narain was constrained to caution the people against the adverse impact of these activities. Around this time also, the National Conference was converted to the Indian National Congress in January 1965; and this had deepened the suspicions of some of the Kashmiris.

In the country at large, as a result of the Chinese Aggression against India, the economy had suffered to a considerable extent and the nation was yet to recover. On the political side, some of the Sikh leaders demanded division of the Punjab State on linguistic basis and this had led to considerable tension. The first Indian Prime Minister, Jawaharlal Nehru, had passed away on 27 May 1964 and Lal Bahadur Shastri assumed this appointment. In the North-East, insurgency continued unabated. Communal groups in India were retaliating against Pakistani propaganda, by undesirable utterances. Due to all these, the general state of affairs in India and particularly in Kashmir, were perhaps misinterpreted by Pakistan as a situation of increasing chaos and loss of control that could be taken advantage of.

As far as Pakistan was concerned, considerable economic progress had been achieved, both due to agricultural production and industrial growth. Significant economic assistance was being received. Added to this was the massive military aid received from United States. General Ayub Khan, the Commander-in-Chief of the Pakistan Army, who had come into power as a result of a military coup, renewed his efforts at obtaining Pakistani control over Kashmir. Pakistan not only improved its relations with China but also started attempts to better relations with the Soviet Union. Zulfikar Ali Bhutto, the Foreign Minister pursued vigorously the pro-China policies of Pakistan, taking advantage of the adverse Sino-Indian relations. However, despite all these favourable factors, Pakistan had its own internal problems, particularly lack of cohesiveness between its two wings, i.e., West and East. The East Pakistanis, who constituted 55 percent of the nation's population felt dominated by the West, neglected and exploited as second rate citizens. Separatist tendencies among the East Pakistanis created considerable anxiety to the rulers in the West. In the general elections held in the country, based on the so-called Basic Democracies System (which was really of an extremely limited democratic nature), although Ayub had won, Miss Jinnah, the combined opposition candidate, received a significant vote; and this also had shaken the rulers. There was considerable agitation for greater political freedom in the country. In addition to all these, Pakistan's efforts at the United Nations to get a favourable response on the Kashmir issue did not meet with success. The Indian Foreign Minister M. C. Chagla stated at the United Nations that the two basic United Nations resolutions of 1948 and 1949 "were conditional and contingent on Pakistan vacating its aggression and the condition have not been complied with. The condition not having been complied with and the basis having disappeared, these resolutions are no longer binding on us". Further, both the United States and the Soviet Union felt that the Kashmir question had to be resolved by bilateral talks between the two sides and that an agreement could not be imposed from outside. It would appear that Pakistan, having been disappointed at its lack of success on this issue, perhaps started considering by early 1965 that force was the only means to achieve her aim, as would be evident from the subsequent events.

To start with, Pakistan engineered a large number of incidents along the Ceasefire Line and thus hotted it up. While the number of incidents up to 1961 remained low (maximum in a year 62), during 1962 there were 468, during 1963—354, during 1964—1,522, and during 1965 upto the end of May, there were 1,345 incidents. Later, the UNMOGIP confirmed to the United Nations, of the increasing pressure along the Ceasefire Line by Pakistan. The Indian 15 Corps, under Lieutenant General K.S. Katoch, was responsible for operations in Jammu and Kashmir and had to contend with the situation.

The hawks in Pakistan continued to hallucinate about India's disintegration due to the diversity of its population. They expected the disparate tendencies in India to blossom under the shock of the outcome of the Sino-Indian War. Instead they saw a determined and politically united India emerging out of that fiasco. After the failure of the Indo-Pak 1963 parleys to resolve the Kashmir tangle, Pakistan lost all hope of settling the Kashmir issue through peaceful means. The hawks now convinced themselves that their only hope of acquiring Kashmir was to grab it by force. They calculated that the balance of military power was bound to tilt increasingly in India's favour with military aid from USA and her Western Allies and the implementation of India's First Five Year Defence Plan. They considered that they should act before Mr. Shastri, the new Prime Minister after Nehru's death, could establish himself firmly in the saddle and before India expanded her forces. They considered that the time was opportune for an early military venture. India, on her side, needed time to build her forces and to strengthen the new political leadership. It was imperative for India to avoid any military conflict; so the initiative for military venture, if any, was with Pakistan.

ESCALATION

Kutch

The Rann of Kutch is a vast waste land of about 9,065 square kilometres, in the mid-western part of India. From about May to October every year, it gets covered with water from the Arabian Sea. During the remaining period of year it remains as a semi-desert area, dry but difficult for movement. The area is sparsely populated. According to the pre-partition records available with India, the entire Rann belongs to India. However, Pakistan laid claim for about half the Rann going down to the twenty-fourth parallel.

In early 1965, it was discovered that Pakistani Rangers were sending patrols well inside Indian territory in the Rann of Kutch. India protested and at the same time intensified its own patrolling. Repeated protests by India had no effect on Pakistan. On the other hand, on 9 April 1965, Pakistani forces in Brigade strength attacked Sardar Post near the old ruined Fort of Kanjarkot. As India only had Police forces in the area, some of these were overrun by the regular troops of Pakistan.

India decided to reinforce the area with some of her own regular forces, created a Kilo Sector under Major General P. O. Dunn, and started organising the defence of the Rann (Op Ablaze). On 24 April 1965, Pakistan launched a divisional-sized attack under Major General Tikka Khan, using Patton tanks and field guns. Despite the disadvantages under which Indian forces were fighting, the Pakistani attack was contained with considerable casualties to the Pakistani troops. It has to be remembered that no preparations were ever made by India to send regular troops into this area and that the Indian forces had to depend on long and difficult lines of communication, while the Pakistanis were at a great advantage in this respect being well-served by communications.

Subsequently, a ceasefire was arrived at. It was also decided with the help of Britain, that status quo ante would be restored in accordance with an Agreement signed on 30 June 1965, pending arbitration of the problem by a three-man Tribunal. The Chairman was to be named by the Secretary General of the United Nations if the parties concerned could not select one, while each side would name one member. However, implementation could not be carried out, owing to Pakistani machinations in Kashmir.

It appeared that Pakistan put to test its newly acquired equipment from the United States and seems to have been enamoured with her achievements, particularly, the initial success in the Rann. Later events also indicated that Pakistan was testing the will and resolve of the Indian Government.

Kargil

As part of her continued pressure on the ceasefire line in Kashmir, Pakistan planned to cut off the Indian line of communications to Ladakh in the Kargil area. On 16 May 1965, Pakistani units attacked some Indian forces along the cease fire line, in order to gain dominance of the road going to Leh from Srinagar. Inaction on the part of India would have meant that all the forces in Ladakh, facing the Chinese would have been completely cut off. Thus a counter attack was launcher by the local Indian Brigade (121) and the Pakistanis driven out. This attack was over extremely difficult terrain under inclement weather conditions. In this counter-attack, Pakistani troops suffered considerable casualties. The line of communication to Leh was thus cleared.

Infiltration—Operation GIBRALTAR

During the period 5-10 August 1965, Indian troops in Kashmir discovered infiltrators in columns of about 600 in strength or more, in different sectors across the ceasefire line, all over Kashmir. In some areas, they had captured lightly held out-posts while in other cases, they had come fairly deep. The infiltrating columns covered almost all the strategically important sectors such as Punch, Uri, Tithwal and so on. Some of these managed to isolate certain Indian positions while others indulged in sabotage.

Captured prisoners and documents revealed a deliberate plan by Pakistan to take over Kashmir by a guerrilla assault, along with an expected uprising within the State. A special force of thirty thousand men known as "Gibraltar Force" was organised for the purpose, under Major General Akhtar Hussain Malik. General Officer Commanding 12 Division. This comprised ten forces, each of six units of five companies each. Each company was commanded by a regular officer and the companies comprised personnel of the regular army as well as irregulars. They were equipped with automatic weapons and light support weapons. The force was trained in different camps, in special operations. They received training in infiltration, sabotage, ambushes and raids. Reports indicated that Chinese Communist instructors had helped them in their training. Much of the equipment bore Pakistan Ordnance Factory markings, while some of it even had Chinese markings. Many of the personnel were in Mujahideen dress while some of them were wearing Pakistan military uniforms. The tasks given to the infiltrators included destruction of bridges with a view to disrupting lines of communications, ambushing of convoys, raids on military headquarters, installations and administrative centres and sabotage in general with a view to paralysing the Administration. They were to distribute arms and ammunition to local civilians, enrol them as Razakars, train and indoctrinate them and encourage them to rise in rebellion against the Government.

Although Pakistan denied any complicity in the infiltration and termed it as an uprising within Kashmir by the locals, there was absolutely clear cut evidence of their involvement. This was confirmed by the head of the United Nations Military Observer Group, General R.H. Nimmo, in a number of reports despatched to the United Nations. U Thant, the United Nations Secretary General, stated in the Security Council on 3 September 1965 that "the series of violations that began on 5 August were to a considerable extent in subsequent days in the form of armed men, generally not in uniform, crossing the CFL from the Pakistan side for the purpose of armed action on the Indian side".

Interrogation of some of the infiltrators revealed that the plans for the attack were completed before the end of May, a month before the Rann of Kutch Agreement. Further, President Ayub himself had addressed the force commanders at Murree in the second week of July.

It was evident that the Pakistani strategy was that the guerrillas would infiltrate into Kashmir and engineer a revolt. Once the State Government was paralysed and collapsed, regular forces whose help would have been sought in the name of a Revolutionary Council, would intervene in Kashmir. However, Indian forces reacted speedily and eliminated many of the infiltrators or captured them. Most of the groups dissipated or dispersed. The expected revolt did not materialize and the infiltration operation was frustrated by the Indian forces. The local population fully supported the Indian forces, by way of providing intelligence, administrative support and even support of operations, such as tracking infiltrators and apprehending them.

It was discovered that most of the personnel of the Gibraltar Force were from outside Kashmir. It was also noticed that a so-called freedom radio 'Sada-i-Kashmir' (Voice of Kashmir) was really operating from Pakistan Occupied Kashmir. The Pakistani press even used to publish details of operations, which could only have been done with previous knowledge of plans. Pakistani complicity is further supported by the fact that they were averse to the publication of United Nations Observer's reports by the Secretary General. It is clear that Pakistan wanted to disown responsibility for the infiltration, in the same manner as she did in the earlier 1947 attack. At the same time, India could not get the United Nations to brand Pakistan as the aggressor, as the organisation was more concerned with restoring peace at the time.

Even as the infiltration by the Pakistani forces was being dealt with, on 14 August 1965, regular troops of Pakistan Army in battalion strength launched an attack opposite Bhimber and captured some Indian posts on the hill range to the North. Along with this, there was continuous shelling of Indian positions. This attack by the Pakistanis put the road communication from Jammu to Punch in jeopardy. Pakistani artillery also continuously shelled Indian positions in all the major sectors of the cease fire line, perhaps to encourage and support operations by their infiltrators. It may be mentioned that although a large number of infiltrators were either killed or captured, some who had disappeared into the countryside were still able to interfere with the Indian lines of communications. It was also apparent that the infiltrators continued to receive support from bases inside Pakistan Occupied Kashmir.

Capture of Hajipir

Towards the later part of August, it became clear that unless the bases from which the infiltrators were receiving support were effectively dealt with, the infiltrators would continue to harass Indian forces. It was, therefore, decided that the strategic Hajipir Pass in the Pakistan-occupied area opposite Uri, should be captured, to eliminate the threat to Uri. This was at a height of about 2,600 metres and strongly held by the Pakistanis. The approaches were over much higher features and extremely difficult. However, in a daring night operation, 68 Indian Brigade under its dynamic Commander Brigader Z.C. Bakshi, captured the Pass by a series of outflanking movements, on 10 September.

Similar operations were launched in the Tithwal Sector to capture an important hill feature, Pir Saheba,

Capture of Chhamb

Chhamb is a village which lies in the plains area to the West of Chenab River. The Pakistan Grand Trunk road going from Lahore to Peshawar is just to the South of this area, across the border. Gujarat town lies along this road opposite Chhamb. North of Chhamb is the Kalidhar Range, the first range of hills overlooking the plains. Kalidhar Range itself dominates the Indian line of communication from Jammu to Poonch, running along a valley to the North. At Akhnoor, an old Class 18 bridge existed, across which tanks could not be taken at that time. Tanks had to be ferried across the Chenab River. The area of Chhamb was held by the Indian Army with about a battalion supported by a few tanks.

On 1 September 1965, the Pakistanis attacked this area with 7 Division under Major General Yahya Khan (Operation GRAND SLAM). This was supported by an armoured brigade and heavy artillery. Against the light opposition that they encountered, the Pakistanis were able to capture this position without much difficulty. Efforts by the Indians to build up further forces in the area failed, as they were somewhat surprised by the strength and place of the attack. However, by their gallant action, the Indian forces prevented the Pakistanis from further advancing into the hills.

The attack on Chhamb was carried out mainly from across the International Border; with a subsidiary threat from across the cease fire line to the West As usual, Pakistan had initially denied having crossed the International Border to the East and termed the operation as one launched by the Pakistan Occupied Kashmir (POK) forces.

The Chief Military Observer, General Nimmo, confirmed that the "border had indeed been crossed by Pakistani regular forces". Subsequently, Pakistani troops occupied the entire area upto the Munawar Wali Tawi River. It should be noted that, from the trend of past operations, the Indians had not expected the Pakistanis to cross the International Border, but to confine their operations to the CFL.

The Pakistanis continued their advance towards Akhnoor and captured the important village of Jaurian on 5 September, which is clearly across the International Border. Subsequently, they continued their advance towards Akhnoor and reached a point, only 6 kilometres short of the border town. However, due to Indian resistance, they were unable to capture Akhnoor. Loss of this area by the Indians would have cut off the complete forces to the West of Akhnoor, right up to and including Poonch (about a Division strength). In this operation, the Indians had to use the Air Force to support the ground troops in stalling the Pakistani advance.

Despite a major attack launched by regular forces of considerable strength of Pakistan, in addition to the infiltration operations by the Gibraltar Force, the Indian attitude had all along been conciliatory. India had assured the United Nations that it would act with restraint and that it would respect the Ceasefire Agreement, if Pakistan also similarly responded. However, Pakistan would not respond to the appeal for peace even by the United Nations Secretary General. Instead, the Pakistani Commander-in-Chief (General Mohammed Musa) sent a message to his troops on 5 September: "You have got your teeth into him. Bite deeply and deeply until he is destroyed. And destroy him immediately, God willing." On the same day, Pakistani aircraft attacked some Indian installations in the Amritsar area. Under these conditions, India could no longer restrain herself and allow herself to be further humiliated. Any inaction or inadequate action on her part would have resulted in dangerous consequences to her vital interests. Something significant had to be done immediately, to counter the escalating Pakistani threat

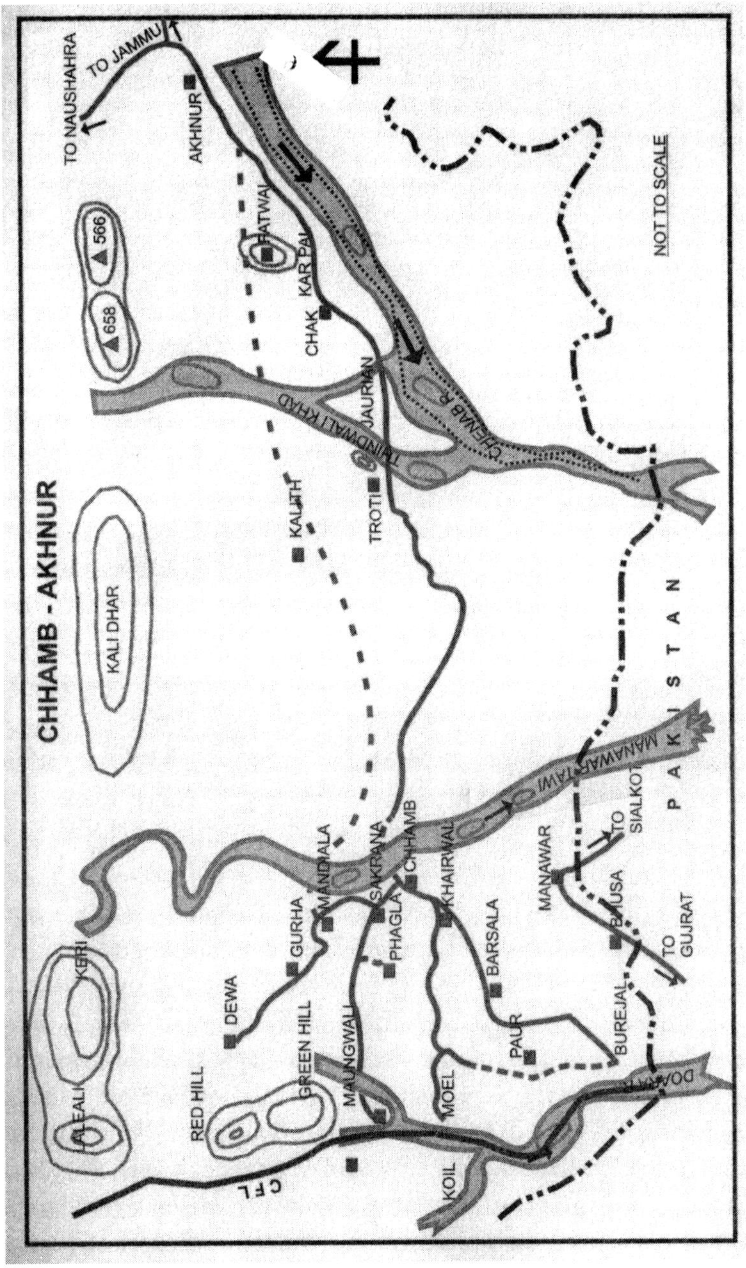

Map 1: Chhamb – Akhnur Sector

TOPOGRAPHY, RELATIVE STRENGTHS AND STRATEGY

Topography

Before describing the course of the war, it would be useful to understand the topography (of the whole plains area of operations, that of Jammu and Kashmir), as it existed at the time. The Cease Fire Line (CFL) coming down from the Himalayas in the North, through the hills of Jammu and Kashmir, terminated in the area West of Chhamb, at a place called Burejal. From there on, the International Border between Pakistan and India runs Eastward through the plains, along the old boundary of Jammu and Kashmir State with India upto a place called Bamial on the Ravi River. From there onwards, it turns South and Southwest towards the Rajasthan desert. It passes through the fertile plains of Punjab, but there is really no natural boundary as such, except that in some areas, the Ravi River and in some others the Sutlej River, run along the boundary. After passing through Northern Rajasthan, the boundary turns South-westward, and after going through the desert, ends in the area of Kutch. Chenab, Ravi, Beas and Sutlej are the major rivers in the area under consideration, and run from North-East to South-West.

The plain areas on either side are generally well served by road communications and rail communications. The main Grand Trunk road from Delhi to Peshawar passes through Amritsar and Lahore. Certain canal networks, taking off from the headworks on the major rivers, and passing through both East and West Punjab, existed, even before Partition of the country. However, a major development after the Partition, was the construction of a major canal from Marala Headworks on the Chenab river, going South and Southeast to Bambanwala on the Ravi river, thus linking Chenab with Ravi and carrying the waters of the former into the latter river. From Bambanwala on the Ravi, another canal, known as the Ichhogil canal (Bambanwala-Ravi-Bedian Link—BRB) runs Southwards to Bedian,

Kasur and some distance beyond. This canal generally goes parallel to the Indo-Pakistan border and is a sizeable obstacle. Pakistan developed a defence network based on this canal. Another canal was under construction from Suleimanki Headworks towards the Southwest to Fort Abbas, which runs more or less parallel to the border and is also a formidable obstacle. From these canals, a number of subsidiary canals were also constructed. On the Indian side, no such canals or defence obstacles were constructed up to this time. The present extensive network of Ditch-cum-Bund obstacles on both sides of the border came up after the 1965 war. The general area on either side of the border comprised fertile plains. The major cities on either side, namely Lahore and Amritsar were more or less at equal distance from the border (about 25 to 30 kilometres). There were other fairly large sized towns such as Sialkot, Shakargarh and Kasur on the Pakistan side and Jammu, Pathankot, Ferozepur and Fazilka on the Indian side. There were many smaller and fairly well developed towns on either side, in many cases, close to the border.

The most important strategic area of India and Pakistan lay in the Bari Doab where Lahore and Amritsar, the twin cities were the most prestigious objectives. Lahore is less than 30 kilometres from the border. It was an obvious objective for India and Pakistan had added to its defence potential by constructing the formidable obstacle of the Ichhogil Canal. Amritsar, on the Indian side, is about 25 kilometres from the border and is a communication centre matching Lahore. The capture of Amritsar by Pakistan would open up the direct route to the Beas bridge. It would threaten to seal the fate of the Indian forces in the Amritsar-Khalra areas with disastrous consequences to the Indian side. Pakistan could hope to base her defences on the Beas river and then advance north to cut the then only road link between India and the State of Jammu & Kashmir. The communication network and the irrigation system was a legacy of the British Raj. There were three major roads connecting important objectives in the Bari Doab on either side of the border.

(a) GT axis provides a direct and shortest access between Lahore and Amritsar.

(b) Amritsar-Bhikkiwind cross-roads to Barki-Lahore. This provides a near frontal approach to Lahore while, for a force coming from the Pakistan side, it provides a flanking approach to Amritsar and its rear areas.

(c) Amritsar-Bhikkiwind-Khemkaran-Kasur-Lahore. A subsidiary road links Khem Karan to Beas/Jandiala on the GT road via Patti. This approach had minimum obstacles against any Pakistani advance towards Amritsar or the Beas bridge. It led the Pakistani advancing forces to the rear areas of Indian forces deployed along the border on the Barki and GT axes. The small township of Khem Karan assumed military significance as it blocked this approach from Kasur towards Bhikkiwind and Patti. Any major enemy advance along the Kasur-Khem Karan axis could prove dangerous with its potential to unhinge 11 Corps from a flank, while threatening its soft rear areas. If successful, Pakistan could isolate 11 Corps from the rest of the Indian Army with dire consequences. This route provided the longest approach to Lahore from the Indian side and had a number of obstacles.

A major point is the configuration of what is known as the Shakargarh bulge. Owing to the lie of the border, this bulge juts into the apex of the triangle formed at the place where the border running from West to East turns Southwards in the general area of Bamial. This bulge has considerable strategic significance in that, from here Pakistan can launch attacks to sever Jammu and Kashmir from the rest of India.

Geographically, Pakistan had a number of strategic disadvantages and tactical advantages vis-a-vis India. Pakistan lacks strategic depth in West Pakistan where no vital area was out of reach of the IAF. All major rail and road communications between Lahore and Jhelum and the canal headworks over the Chenab and Jhelum are outflanked by India from the territory of Jammu province. Karachi was the only port in West Pakistan through which she could import the war material from abroad to support her military operations. The only

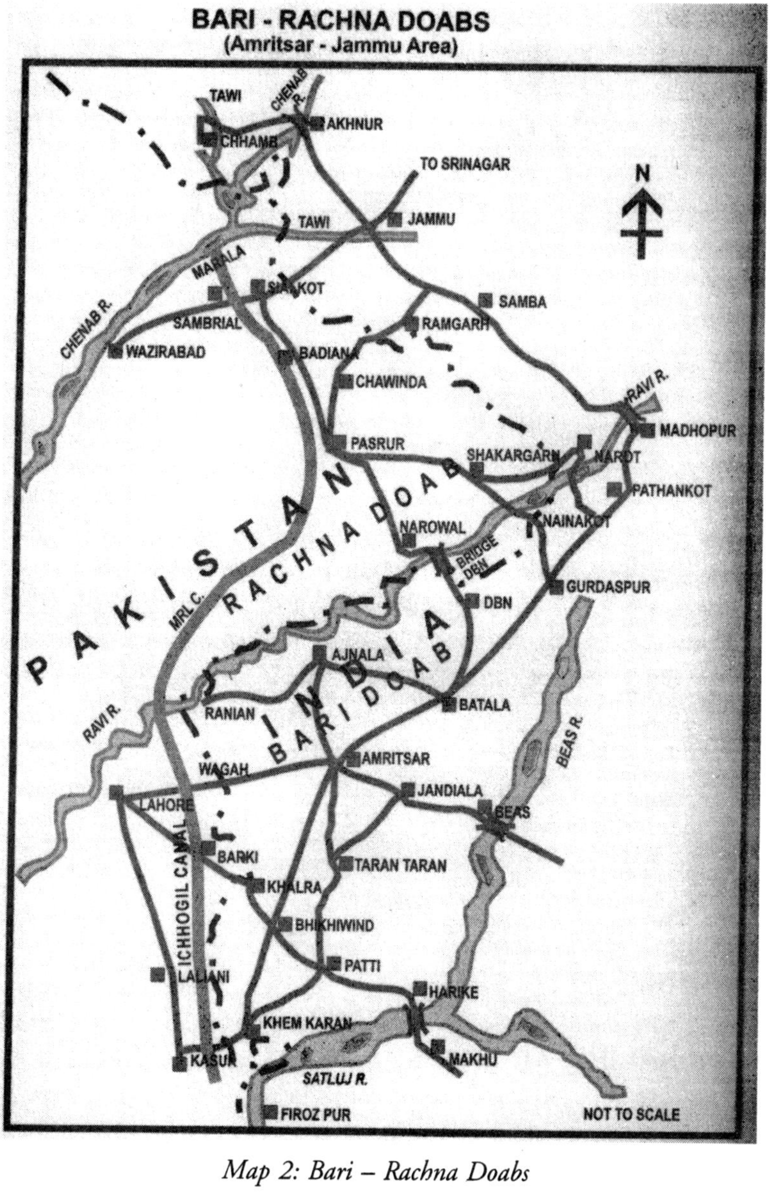

Map 2: Bari – Rachna Doabs

rail and road link between Karachi and the Punjab was liable to interruption by Indian raiding parties especially in the Rahim Yar Khan area.

Pakistan's advantage was that her cantonments in West Pakistan were located close to the international boundary so her troops could reach their operational areas in a short time to achieve surprise. Indian troops, on the other hand, would take much longer to reach their operational areas, due to the long travel time from the distant cantonments. Pakistan had the additional advantage of operating on interior lines which facilitated a quick shift of troops between the Lahore and Sialkot sectors. The movement, of course, was restricted to the then only bridge over the Ravi near Lahore.

Kashmir, the bone of contention, was the main factor in the strategic planning of both sides. The Jammu & Kashmir State was at an extremity of India, and Srinagar was connected to the Pathankot rail-head by a long and tenuous road. The road crossed the Chenab at Ramban in a landslide-prone area and ran over the Banihal pass which was snowbound during winter. Pakistan was better placed for communications to Pakistan Occupied Kashmir. Its cantonments were suitably located to reinforce any area in Jammu & Kashmir at short notice. This was an important aspect for troop build-up in view of the restrictions on troop reinforcements under the Karachi Agreement. While Pakistan could locate troops on its own territory for quick induction into Jammu & Kashmir, India could not do so, as any reinforcements could not be located beyond the Pathankot-Madhopur area. From Pathankot, the move forward to Jammu and beyond took considerable time.

The Ichhogil canal formed a major obstacle. While the Pakistanis could cross it in their own territory, Indian forces intending an advance to Lahore had to execute an opposed crossing over it. By its very nature, it could form a formidable defence line for either side if they could occupy the bank on their side. As an obstacle, the canal could be divided into three distinct parts. The first part, from the source to the GT road inclusive, had steep brick-lined banks. The second part covered the Khalra-Barki axis where the Pakistanis could flood the area by cutting the banks. The third portion included Bedian to the canal junction with the Sutlej where the various aqueducts could be used for crossing the canal.

The border from the Sialkot area to Madhopur generally runs west to east. Any advance in the Rachna Doab could thus follow the grain of the country without involving any water crossing. A number of dry streams run in the area from the north east to the south west. Pakistan had linked the Chenab with the Ravi by the Marala-Ravi Link Canal (MRLC) as an irrigation-cum-defence channel against any deep advance towards its National Highway in the Gujranwala-Wazirabad area. The sector was suitable for tank operations and an advance from north to south or vice versa faced few natural obstacles. In this sector, the Dera Baba Nanak (DBN) rail-road bridge offered an indirect approach against the Indian defences in the Amritsar area and also an approach to outflank the Pakistani defences in the Sialkot Sector. However it involved the crossing of the Ravi in the initial stages.

In the Rachna Doab sector, Sialkot and Jammu are important towns. They are about 15 kilometres apart and were linked by road and rail. The rail track had been lifted on either side of the border. Sialkot was linked to Narowal opposite DBN via Pasrur by a rail and road network. Pakistan could cut the Jammu-Pathankot road which ran within easy striking distance of Pakistani forces, opposite the Samba area with serious consequences to the logistics and security of the Indian forces in Jammu & Kashmir. India, in turn, could threaten the lifeline of Pakistan by launching a deep offensive to cut the Peshawar-Lahore rail/ road network in the Wazirabad area. India could thus split the Pakistani forces into three parts—the Bari Doab, Rachna Doab, and west of the Chenab River.

In Punjab, Pakistan had the advantage of operating on interior lines in the Lahore and Sialkot sectors. She could shift troops quickly from one sector to the other by rail and road. The Ravi bridge near Lahore was the only bottleneck. Similarly, she could shift troops from the Chhamb sector to the Sialkot sector quickly over the Marala Headworks. India had to operate in the Bari and Rachna Doab on exterior lines over the Madhopur road-bridge on the Ravi involving longer moves. While any east-west advance in the Lahore-Amritsar sector involved crossings over numerous canals, India could advance in the Sialkot sector from Jammu along the grain of the country. In addition, the terrain in Sialkot sector was tankable providing space for manoeuvre. Any east-west advance from the DBN to Narowal and Pasrur would envelop the Pakistan forces in the Sialkot sector from a flank and rear, though it would have to cross a number of sandy nalas and would initially involve an opposed crossing of the Ravi.

The desert region of Rajasthan and Sind permitted only minor operations where India could undertake to interfere with the Pakistani railroad system in the Rahim Yar Khan area. Similarly operations of marginal importance were possible in the Barmer sector. These operations were unlikely to seriously affect the outcome of war.

Another factor in favour of Pakistan was that she faced no threat from any of her neighbours except India. She, in fact, expected help from China in a war against India. She was also hopeful of getting arms and ammunition from Turkey and Iran, the Islamic members of CENTO. Even though Pakistan had a boundary dispute with Afghanistan, yet she could count on the Islamic States in the Middle East to pressure Afghanistan to desist from any hostile act against Pakistan. So Pakistan could plan a single-front war while India had to be ready for a two-front war against China and Pakistan.

Geographically, India had a distinct advantage as her communication system ran vertical to the Pakistani border except in the Madhopur-Jammu Sector where the road ran parallel and within striking distance of the Pakistani Shakargarh area. India's handicap was the long time needed to concentrate her forces along the Pakistani border. The PAF reach was limited and India could move troops by rail or road by day to destinations from where they could reach their deployment areas by night, without much interference from the PAF.

In the later stages of World War II, the Indian Army had got used to operating against the enemy without much consideration of the hostile air action. Later with the induction of high speed aircraft, it was accepted that the Indian air defence equipped with L 60 Bofors gun was not effective against the fast moving jet fighters. The Indian Army had not been exposed to any hostile air activity during the 1947-48 Jammu & Kashmir War, or the Sino-Indian War. Over the years, the level of close air support or battle cooperation training between the IAF and the Army had thus taken a back seat. The role of air defence artillery was accepted as merely deterrent and most of the air defence units had been converted to the Territorial Army (TA). The IAF worked on the doctrine that the Air Force could not provide assured close support or air defence to ground troops until it had achieved air supremacy. Support to the ground troops in the initial stages of war was thus minimal and chancy. The air defence (AD) guns were not available to the advancing troops on the first day of the war as AD regiments (TA) were not mobilised in time.

Considering the international situation and logistical limitations, both India and Pakistan realised that a war between them would be of short duration. The US and USSR were anxious to prevent a war between India and Pakistan, as China, their common enemy, could be the only gainer in such an event. They could apply pressure on India and Pakistan as both depended on the Western World for their war material. India needed food in addition to weapons, while Pakistan was absolutely dependent on the US for the replenishment of war material. As soon as open hostilities started, the US stopped war material supplies to both countries which hurt Pakistan more than India. India had started manufacturing certain types of ammunition. Thus, the war strategy of both was for an early military decision or at least quick territorial gains before the cessation of hostilities. The national aim of Pakistan was to acquire the territory of the Jammu & Kashmir State, especially the province of Kashmir, while India's object was to maintain status quo in Jammu & Kashmir.

Pakistan's purpose was to grab Jammu & Kashmir by force; so the degree of success or failure in Jammu & Kashmir was of primary concern to her. In case of war, it was in India's interest not only to defend the CFL but to improve her defence posture by capturing areas of strategic value to her inside Pakistan Occupied Kashmir. Pakistan's object was to grab maximum territory in Jammu & Kashmir including Srinagar. As approaches to Srinagar Valley in the high mountains get snowbound in winter, Pakistan had to initiate operations in the summer months only. The main approach to Srinagar from Pakistan was along the Muzaffarabad-Uri road. A secondary approach was from Muzaffarabad via Tithwal. As the Kishenganga had no road bridge, the scope of operations along this approach was limited. Another area of tactical importance was the Hajipir Bulge which was linked by mule and foot tracks to the Pakistani road heads at Kotli, Rawalakot, Bagh and Palandhri. Operations from the Bulge could be launched against the Poonch, Uri and Gulmarg sectors. Considering the nature of ground, communications and the defences, conventional offensive operations did not offer the promise of an early or easy success.

In the Jammu province, the road system was better and operations were feasible throughout the year. The Akhnoor bridge offered an attractive objective and Pakistan could hope to capture it by a quick armour-cum-infantry thrust via Chhamb. Pakistan could assemble forces in her territory swiftly for offensive operations against the Chhamb and Jammu sector without violating the Karachi Agreement. India was handicapped by the time required to move troops from Pathankot, the nearest Indian border cantonment and rail head, and limitations of the Akhnoor bridge for the move of medium tanks to Chhamb. The Karachi agreement had laid restrictions on both India and Pakistan not to improve defences or reinforce their forces inside Jammu & Kashmir which were to remain as on 1 January 1949.

Another area of attraction for the Pakistanis was the Pathankot-Jammu road. While Pakistan could assemble troops in her territory for swift operations against the road, India could not induct additional troops into Jammu & Kashmir State area without violating the Karachi Agreement. In the event of Pakistan cutting this road,

India would have no choice but to conduct operations to open the only road to ensure logistical support to her forces in Jammu & Kashmir. Any Indian offensive against the Narowal-Pasrur Sector would not only pose a threat to the Pakistani life-line in the Wazirabad area but automatically ensure depth and security to the Indian troops' life-line to Jammu & Kashmir.

Kargil was another area where the Pakistanis could interfere with Indian communications with Leh. Kargil town was in Indian hands but the Pakistanis occupied the high ground overlooking Kargil and the Srinagar-Leh road. The availability of the road gave India a logistical advantage over Pakistan who had to supply her forces in the Kargil area over pony tracks from Skardu.

RELATIVE STRENGTHS AND DEPLOYMENT OF FORCES

While formulating the plans, the military leadership has to evaluate relative capabilities and intentions of the opponents. One has to identify the strategic areas which must be defended adequately and simultaneously select areas for capture. The plans must be designed not only for material gains but for moral and psychological effect and as powerful levers for bargaining during peace negotiations. Wars invariably start with the conflicting expectations of adversaries. The contradictory optimism is brought about by wishful thinking, faulty assessments of enemy capabilities and intentions, expectations of intervention by allies, wrong appreciation of internal turmoil and the level of morale in the opponent's camp.

The relative strength of Indian and Pakistan armed forces in 1965 shows that Pakistan was stronger than India in armour, fire power and mobility. The PAF had superior aircraft against a numerically larger IAF. Pakistan, of course, had a marked numerical inferiority in infantry which is the decisive arm in mountain warfare. India, of course, had a numerical superiority in infantry, artillery and aircraft. Paradoxical as it seems, it is invariably the weaker side which initiates a warlike action. Realising her inability to grab Kashmir by a direct involvement of her armed forces, Pakistan opted for guerrilla operations in Kashmir to achieve her purpose. She intended to keep the guerrilla operation at a level of escalation hoping that India would limit her counteractions to combat the guerrillas on the Indian side of the CFL. She was wishful of a mass uprising of the local population in support of the guerrillas. If India reacted by moving large forces to Kashmir, she planned for major offensive operations in the Bari Doab against the 'thinned' forces in Indian Punjab.

Pakistan

At the time of the war (September 1965), Pakistan had a total strength of two Corps Headquarters, two Armoured Divisions, seven Infantry Divisions, some Independent Infantry Brigades and a large number of Para-Military Forces, all controlled by GHQ at Rawalpindi. Except for one division (14), which was deployed in East Pakistan, the remainder of the Forces were all located in West Pakistan. Within West Pakistan, the deployment was 12 Infantry Division (equivalent of-more than two divisions) with Headquarters at Murree looking after the Occupied Kashmir Area, 15 Infantry Division with an additional brigade in the Sialkot area, 10 Infantry Division in the Lahore area, 11 Infantry Division in the Kasur area and Independent Brigades at Suleimanki and Badin. 8 Infantry Division was deployed on the North-West frontier. 1 Armoured Division (peace time location Kharian) and 7 Infantry Division (peace time location Peshawar) grouped together, were to be the strike force and 6 Armoured Division (location Gujranwala) was a reserve formation. Headquarters 1 Corps, located at Kharian was to control the Sialkot front, while Headquarters 4 Corps located at Lahore was to control the Lahore front. A strike Corps Headquarters was conceived but was yet to be formed. Pakistan also had a large body of irregular forces well armed.

After the Kutch operation, the Pakistani forces continued to remain in their forward concentration area, within striking distance of the border. Most of them had not returned to their peace time cantonments. Further, it has to be noted that 7 Infantry Division was committed in the Chhamb-Jaurian operation. The strike force was, therefore, somewhat disturbed, but re-constituted with 11 Infantry Division having been grouped with 1 Armoured Division.

As a result of considerable arms aid received from United States of America, the Pakistan armed forces had the most modem equipment of the time, available to them. They had also carried out extensive training and trials and reorganised themselves. Consequently, the formations and units were streamlined and were in a high state of preparedness for war. After the launching of operations GIBRALTAR and GRANDSLAM, they also maintained a fairly high degree of alert.

Pakistan's plan of war was briefly as under:

(a) **Jammu & Kashmir State.** Induct guerrillas under Army control from Kargil to Chhamb along the whole length of the CFL to create turmoil and disrupt civil authority. Pakistan had earmarked troops to move into Indian Kashmir in case the guerrillas created a favourable situation in Srinagar and its surrounding areas. The guerrilla induction and operations were planned for a long-drawn-out campaign. 12 Pakistan Division exercised command and control over the extensive deployment of troops in Jammu & Kashmir including Azad Kashmir troops and para-military forces along the CFL.

(b) **Sialkot Sector.** Defend Sialkot-Narowal-Jassar Sector with one infantry division supported by adequate armour. The newly raised armoured division was to be located in Pasrur area as reserve.

(c) **Lahore Sector.** This sector covered the area from exclusive Jassar to inclusive Hussainiwala. 10 Pakistan Division was responsible to guard the GT road and Khalra-Barki axes. A newly raised 11 Pakistan Division, was responsible for guarding the Khem Karan-Kasur and Ferozepur-Kasur axes. Pakistan's strategic strike force consisting of 1 Armoured Division and 7 Infantry Division was tasked to capture the rail-cum-road bridge at Beas and thereafter to cut Amritsar off from the rear. The offensive was to be launched after the confirmation that the Indian 1 Armoured Division was not in the Amritsar sector.

(d) **Sulaimanke Sector.** One infantry brigade was earmarked to defend the Pakistani enclave covering the canal head works. The area south of Sulaimanke was the responsibility of the Desert Rangers. In addition, Pakistan had deployed one infantry brigade in a defensive role in the Barmer Sector.

Pakistan had one corps headquarters and a new corps headquarters had been planned for raising. Its raising was postponed in early 1965 to suit the whims of Field Marshal Ayub Khan, who did not wish to promote the approved General.

As a result of the deployment in Punjab during the Kutch operations, General Musa recommended raising two new divisions and a corps headquarters. Due to dilatory bureaucratic procedures, Pakistan went to war without the second corps headquarters and the two divisions.

India

On the other hand, India had to plan her strategy on a two front basis with China as the Number 1 enemy. India appreciated that considering the overall situation, she did not have adequate forces to face a Pakistani offensive in Punjab. This was brought home to India during the Kutch affair. So India undertook to restore military balance by raising a corps headquarters and three infantry divisions on 1 April 1965. These had not completed their raisings when Pakistan unleashed "Op Gibraltar".

At this time, India had three Corps Headquarters, one Armoured Division, one Independent Armoured Brigade, and eight Infantry Divisions available for operations against Pakistan. Three Divisions (19, 25 and 10) were committed on a defensive role in Jammu and Kashmir. 26 Infantry Division was responsible for the defence of the Jammu area and 15 Infantry Division the Amritsar area. The other divisions available were 7 and 14 Infantry Divisions located in North India. 4 and 6 Mountain Divisions with basically a role in the mountains were also used in this war. 11 Infantry Division was responsible for operations in Southern Command. Many of these were located well away from the border, in their peace time cantonments. Of the Corps Headquarters, 15 Corps at Udhampur was controlling the operations in Jammu and Kashmir, 11 Corps at Jullundur was responsible for East Punjab and 1 Corps Headquarters was available for offensive operations.

For operations, divisions were initially grouped under Corps Headquarters as under:

(a) **11 Corps**—7 Infantry Division, 15 Infantry Division, 4 Mountain Division and 2 Independent Armoured Brigade.

(b) **1 Corps**—1 Armoured Division, 26 Infantry Division, 14 Infantry Division and 6 Mountain Division.

(c) **15 Corps**—19 Infantry Division, 25 Infantry Division and 10 Infantry Division, was on the defensive in Jammu and Kashmir. In peace time, even 26 Infantry Division, with a basically defensive role was under this Corps.

The Indian plan was as under:

(a) 11 Corps to operate in the Amritsar Sector from DBN to Fazilka both inclusive. Task allotted to 11 Corps was to secure the east bank of the Ichhogil Canal and capture / destroy all the bridges along its entire length in the Bari Doab.

(b) 1 Corps to launch a simultaneous offensive towards Pasrur from the Samba-Ramgarh area. The task was to secure the home bank of MRLC and cause maximum attrition to the Pak forces in the sector. It was considered that the occupation of defences on the Ichhogil and MRLC would substantially reduce any advantage that the Pakistani tanks had over the Indians. It was expected that 1 Indian Armoured Division would have local superiority in numbers over the Pakistani tanks in the initial encounters as the Pakistanis would be forced to check the oncoming rush of Indian tanks with whatever armour they could muster locally. The Indian side was hopeful of inflicting heavy losses on the enemy armour in its penny packet reactions and encounters.

(c) In Jammu & Kashmir State, 15 Corps was to eliminate the guerrillas inside Indian territory and to attack guerrilla bases across the CFL. It was planned to improve the defensive posture along the CFL particularly in Tithwal, Kargil and Hajipir Bulge. In the Hajipir Bulge, the intention was not only to eliminate the guerrilla bases but to establish a road link between our forces in Uri and Poonch.

India had no intention of starting operations against East Pakistan; even though Indian troops were moved forward in that area in case Pakistan chose to create incidents there.

India did not plan to lower her guard against the Chinese but could not gather adequate forces for an offensive in the west without pulling out troops earmarked for tasks against the Chinese. After cautious scrutiny, minimum troops from the Chinese front were moved to the Indo-Pak front to build up an adequate strike force against Pakistan.

Comparative Military Strength

	Pakistan	*India*
Infantry	7 × infantry divisions 250,000 lightly armed militia	9 × infantry divisions* 11 × mountain divisions†
Armour	2 × armoured divisions**	1 × armoured division 1 independent armoured brigade 5 independent armoured squadrons ‡
Artillery	4 × field regiments (SP) 25 × field regiments 10 × medium regiments 1 × heavy regiment	25 × mountain regiments 41 × field regiments 2 para field regiments 10 × medium regiments 1 × heavy regiment 19 light regiments 21 × AD regiments

	Pakistan	*India*
Air Force	2 × bomber squadrons 9 × fighter squadrons (260 aircraft)	4 × bomber squadrons 32 × fighter squadrons (700 aircraft)

* Of these 4 infantry divisions were on reduced strength
** One armoured division was allegedly at 1/3rd of its strength
Total – 9 regiments (Patton); 5 regiments (Sherman); 3 regiments (Chafee)
† most of them were newly-raised, under-strength and not fully-equipped (deployed against the Chinese)
‡ Total – 4 regiments (Centurion); 8 regiments (Sherman); 2 regiments (AMX-13)

Strategy

As mentioned earlier, India always considered that the massive military aid that Pakistan received from the United States of America, in the name of countering the advance of Communism into the Region, would really be used against her (India), to settle the Kashmir problem in her favour. Further, some responsible leaders in Pakistan even talked about the restoration of the old glory of the Mughals, thereby meaning that, one day, they hoped to rule over the entire Sub-Continent again! India's protestations against the induction of sophisticated arms on a very large scale into Pakistan were never understood by the United States and some of the Western Powers, but instead, they leaned towards Pakistan on the Kashmir issue many a time, as they looked at the problem purely from a religious basis. What is even more important to note is that, by supporting Pakistan and involving her in various Western alliances, they were hoping to use Pakistan to serve their own ends.

Having been emboldened by the political, economic and above all military support that Pakistan had been receiving when she attacked in the Kutch area, she subsequently sent a large number of infiltrators into Jammu and Kashmir and when she launched a major attack towards Akhnoor across the International Border with her regular forces India's apprehension came true. Having appreciated the escalating threat from Pakistan, India decided that if her efforts to resolve any outstanding issues with Pakistan by peaceful means failed, her peaceful intentions were misinterpreted as a sign of weakness and if force was used by Pakistan, she would appropriately counter it. Thus, India made it clear that an attack on Kashmir would be treated as an attack on India and that she reserves the right to retaliate wherever she chooses to along the entire border. Further, as Pakistan itself extended the air war into East Punjab, India was under no compulsion to restrict the war to Jammu and Kashmir which was strategically disadvantageous for her. Thus, it was decided to retaliate across the Punjab border also. Keeping such a contingency in view, plans were made by India and now implemented. In this connection, a statement made by Prime Minister Shastri after the Pakistani attack on Chhamb on 1 September 1965, is worth quoting:

> "President Ayub has been talking a great deal about the tanks and other military equipment Pakistan had acquired and had on many occasions boasted that if they decided to march on Delhi, it would be a walk over. The military situation created by Pakistan was such that our forces had no choice but to advance in the Lahore Sector.
>
> Pakistan's attack was so formidable and so swift that we could not afford merely to talk of defending ourselves. We had to take decisive effective action without losing time. The needs of the situation could no longer be answered by local action. We could not afford to endanger the freedom of our country; no country in the world would have allowed its freedom to be threatened as ours was. We have always held fast to the principles of peace, but in the situation that was created, not to act would have been cowardice and sloth. The display of the armed might we saw within our territory could be resisted only with arms."

Keeping in view the near-parity of forces with Pakistan and the ever likely Chinese threat from the North, Indian counter offensive plans envisaged a swift move across the borders into the Pakistani territory, suitably positioning its formations for the inevitable counter attacks by the Pakistanis, and causing maximum possible destruction to the Pakistani armed might; and in the process, knock out her ability to continue aggressive action against India. It was never the intention of India neither to capture Lahore or any major city nor to make any territorial gains with a view to retaining these. To be successful and to ensure that no devastation takes place within Indian territory, the counter offensive had to be launched before Pakistan could do so with her ground forces into East Punjab. Indian suspicions that Pakistan had such plans to carry the war into Punjab, were confirmed later during the war, as would be clear from the narrative.

The Indian plan was:

(a) In Punjab to advance and secure the line of Ichhogil Canal; and thereafter to pose a threat to Lahore, by crossing over the canal in certain places.

(b) From the Jammu side, to advance and cut off Sialkot from Lahore, by driving a wedge in the area North of Gujranwala.

(c) Elsewhere in Jammu and Kashmir and Rajasthan-Kutch area, remain on offensive defence.

(d) Against East Pakistan, remain on a purely defensive posture.

In the West, Indian Army's Western Command under Lieutenant General Harbakhsh Singh had the responsibility for the area from the Ladakh to Northern Rajasthan. From there Southwards, right down to Kutch, the responsibility was that of Southern Command, under Lieutenant General Moti Sagar. Western Command thus had all the three Corps, namely, 15, 11 and 1 under its command. According to the Pakistani Commander-in-Chief, General Mohammed Musa, the likely Indian aims and plans were correctly appreciated by Pakistani General Headquarters. They assessed that India would aim at destroying the fighting power of Pakistan and capture as much territory as she could in West Pakistan. They had, however, appreciated that India would initially attack Sialkot and capture it if possible; otherwise contain it. Concurrently capture Jassar, across the Ravi River.

Having engaged Sialkot and Jassar and hoping to divert Pakistan's attention to these flanks, India was expected to launch her major offensive from the North and East, with a view to cut off the Grand Trunk Road between Wazirabad and Gujranwala and capture Lahore. If not, contain the city of Lahore. They also expected subsidiary offensives at Bedian, Kasur, Suleimanki and in Sind area. As far as East Pakistan was concerned, it was expected that, depending on the course of the operations, Indian forces may advance along the Shillong-Sylhet, Agartala-Comilla and Bongaon-Jessore axes. Pakistani GHQ also expected that in Pakistan Occupied Kashmir, India would launch her main effort against Muzaffarabad from Uri and Tithwal; and advance from Poonch towards Rawalakot/Palandri. Thus it will be seen, that Pakistani GHQ attributed intentions to the Indian forces, much beyond what their military capability permitted

To meet the threat envisaged, Pakistan planned to use her 1 Corps with 6 Armoured Division to prevent an Indian breakthrough from the North and to destroy the Indian forces in the Sialkot-Jassar area. In the East, 4 Corps was to hold the enemy opposite Lahore-Kasur along the Ichhogil canal. Elsewhere, the formations responsible were to be on offensive defence. Pakistan planned to launch her main offensive, with her strike force comprising 1 Armoured Division and 7 Infantry Division, from an area well to the South of Kasur. Although the specific area has not been revealed, it would appear that the offensive was to be launched from general area Abohar-Ganganagar with a view to securing Bhatinda and then developing a further threat beyond. Musa himself was to be in overall control of this operation. However, as 7 Infantry Division of the strike force was committed in the Chhamb-Akhnoor Sector, it later transpired that the plan was changed significantly, both in terms of the force to be used as well as the objective. This would be clear from the course of the narrative.

OPERATIONS IN THE LAHORE SECTOR

Indian Army's 11 Corps under Lieutenant General J.S. Dhillon was given the following tasks:

(a) Destroy any enemy forces which may enter the Punjab and Ganganagar Sector.

(b) Launch three simultaneous thrusts along the axes GT road,

Bhikkiwind-Barki and Bhikkiwind-Khem Karan-Kasur with the aim of securing the east bank of Ichhogil canal from Ichhogil Uttar to its junction with Dipalpur Canal. In the process, capture intact the following bridges on the Ichhogil Canal:

(i) Road bridge at Ichhogil Uttar (Bhaini-Malikpur).

(ii) Road bridge at GT road at Dograi.

(iii) Road and rail bridges over UBDC and Ichhogil Canal at Jallo.

(iv) Barki Bridge over Ichhogil Canal on road Khalra-Lahore.

(c) On completion of (b) above, be prepared to pose a threat to Lahore.

(d) Eliminate Dera Baba Nanak (DBN) enclave, and capture rail-cum-road bridge at DBN, if possible.

(e) To hold the bridgehead at Hussainiwala, contain the Pakistani bridgehead at Sulaimanke and destroy any enemy forces intruding into the Ganganagar Sector.

In the Lahore Sector opposite 11 Corps, Pakistan had planned to hold the length of the Ichhogil Canal with two infantry divisions. Indian intelligence was actually unaware of the raising of 11 Pakistan Division. It had been assessed that 10 Pak Division with four brigades (one each on GT, Barki, Kasur axes and one in reserve) was responsible for the defence of the Lahore Sector. According to General Musa, Pakistan had appreciated that India would employ two or three infantry divisions along GT and Barki axes to capture Lahore. Musa expected India to attempt a breakthrough between Bedian and Kasur using an independent armoured brigade and an infantry division to outflank the Lahore defences. Pakistan anticipated India to attack Kasur from the Ferozepur direction while threatening Sulaimanke from Fazilka. Pakistan had visualised a major Indian attempt to capture Lahore. In addition, they expected an attack by an Indian Division for the capture of the DBN bridge as part of any Indian offensive in the Sialkot sector.

11 Corps had under its command, three Divisions and an Independent Armoured Brigade. These formations were allotted broad tasks as under:

(a) 15 Infantry Division under Major General Niranjan Prasad was to advance from Amritsar Area and secure the line of Ichhogil canal, establish crossings at selected places and then pose a threat to Lahore from the East

(b) 7 Infantry Division under Major General H.K. Sibal was to advance along the Khalra-Barki road (South of Amritsar) and secure certain crossings with a view to threaten Lahore from the South-East. The Division was also to capture Bedian.

(c) 4 Mountain Division under Major General Gurbakhsh Singh was to advance further South along the Khemkaran–Kasur axis and secure the Ichhogil canal; and concurrently form a firm base Southwest of Khemkaran.

(d) Each Infantry Division was to provide a Brigade as Corps reserve for special tasks. In addition, 2 Independent Armoured Brigade was to be Corps reserve.

The advance commenced in the early hours of 6 September and almost all the formations had achieved surprise and secured their initial objectives. Although initially shaken, the Pakistanis, who were already suitably located in their forward concentration areas, reacted sharply. As a result, the Indian formations, which had not consolidated their gains, were forced to fall back, in some cases to the starting points. In a ding-dong battle, some of the formations regained their losses and generally secured the line of Ichhogil canal; while in the Southern area (4 Mountain Divisional Sector) a major battle took place. Field Marshal Ayub declared: "We will not rest until India's guns are silenced forever."

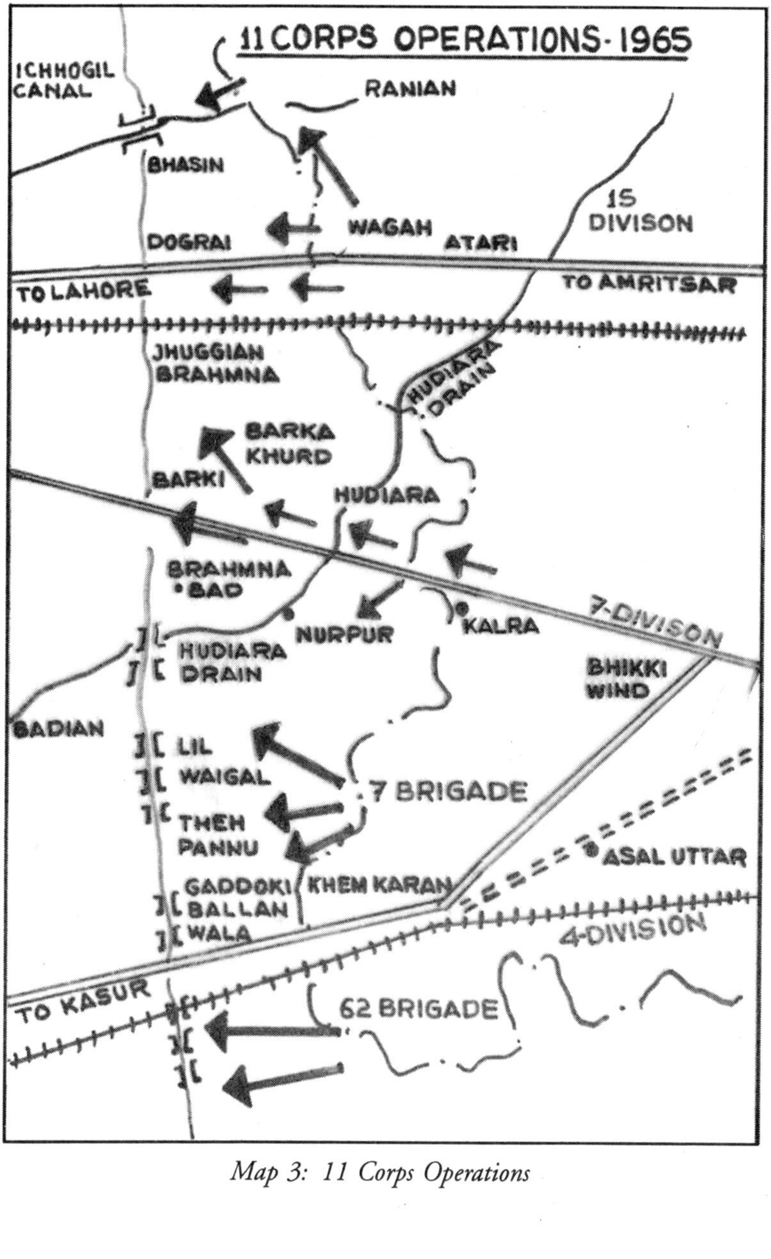

Map 3: 11 Corps Operations

15 Infantry Division Operations

15 Infantry Division gave the task of advancing along the Grand Trunk Road axis and securing the bridge over Ichhogil canal in the Dograi area to 54 Brigade. This Brigade was also to send out a column along the UBDC (Lahore Branch) and secure a bridge linking Jallo. 38 Brigade was assigned the task of securing the Bhaini Dhilwan bridge to the North. 3 JAT of 54 Brigade, under the command of Lieutenant Colonel Desmond Hayde, in a determined move, in the early hours of 6 September, secured the bridge near Dograi and even reached Batapore on the outskirts of Lahore. Enemy tanks attacked forward elements of the battalion, but a troop of 14 Horse (Armoured Regiment. with 15 Infantry Division) arrived in time to prevent the troops being overrun. The rest of the brigade had not fetched up and the battalion came under considerable pressure from the enemy. Subsequently, the battalion was ordered to pull back by the Brigade Commander, Brigadier M.S. Rikh. Accordingly, the battalion occupied the area Dial. 1 JAT of 38 Brigade got to the Bhaini Dhilwan bridge but could not secure it and fell back, reportedly due to fire from tanks and artillery. Both the formations suffered, a number of casualties due to heavy enemy fire including strafing by aircraft. The Divisional Commander reported that he could not carry out any further offensive operations.

Lieutenant General Harbakhsh Singh, along with Lieutenant General Dhillon, visited 15 Infantry Divisional Headquarters and found that the casualties suffered were not so heavy that further offensive action was not possible. He, therefore, directed the Divisional Commander to secure his objective by early next morning. 29 Brigade Commander was ordered to recapture the lost ground and hold fast. General Dhillon sent his GSO-l Lieutenant Colonel Chhajju Ram to be with Brigadier Pritam Singh, till he completed his task. This was done by the early hours of 7 September. The Pakistanis, during their withdrawal, demolished a span of this bridge and made it unusable. 15 Division could not make much headway on 7 September. On the other hand, the Divisional Commander

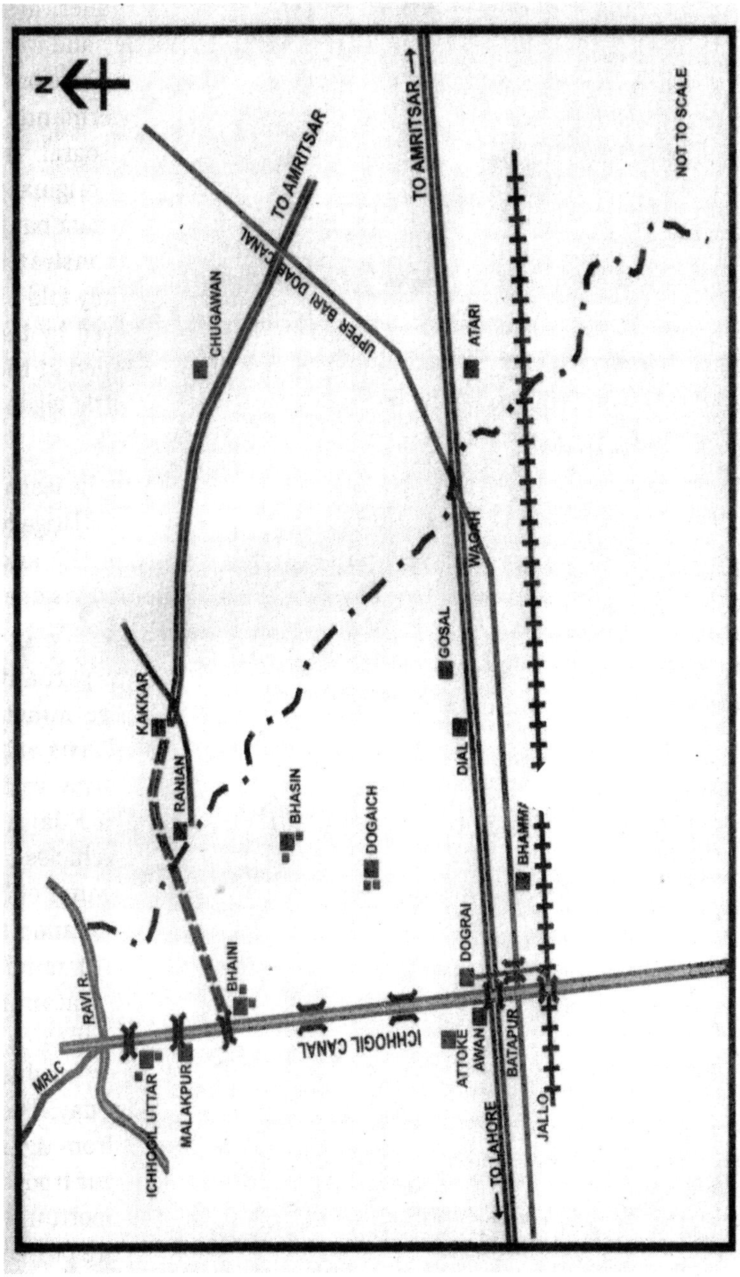

Map 4: Amritsar-Lahore Sector

nearly got caught in a Pakistani ambush. Although he escaped, some of his escorts were captured, as also some documents belonging to the Divisional Commander, which caused considerable embarrassment, as the Pakistanis made use of the information contained for propaganda purposes.

On 7 September, Major General Niranjan Prasad was replaced by Major General Mohinder Singh. Brigadier Rikh who became a casualty was evacuated and subsequently Brigadier Niranjan Singh was put in charge of 54 Brigade. On 11 September, the Pakistanis sent out a strong column of tanks and infantry on the Ranian axis, which forced some infantry of 15 Division to withdraw. 2 Independent Armoured Brigade was moved from the Khemkaran Sector, to restore the situation. Thereafter 96 Brigade captured the Bhaini Dhilwan bridge.

50 Independent Para Brigade under Brigadier A.M.M. Nambiar was placed under command 15 Division on 9 September. This Brigade was employed to capture the rail and road bridges in the Jallo Area on 16/17 September. As the Brigade suffered heavy casualties, Nambiar withdrew his troops further East. As he did this without orders from his Divisional Commander, he was replaced.

On 21/22 September, 15 Infantry Division made a fresh bid to get to the Ichhogil canal. 54 Brigade was to recapture the Dograi area, 38 Brigade was to advance to the canal in its area, and 96 Brigade was to secure the Siphon area to the North. While 38 and 96 Brigades could not secure their objectives, 54 Brigade, was able to succeed, despite heavy odds. Once again 3 JAT, under the inspiring leadership of Lieutenant Colonel Hayde, recaptured Dograi on 22 September and held it against repeated counter attacks by the enemy. Both 3 JAT and the Pakistanis suffered heavy casualties in this battle. For its gallant performance, 3 JAT received three Maha Vir Chakras and a number of other gallantry awards.

7 Infantry Division Operations

Major General H.K. Sibal, General Officer Commanding 7 Infantry

Division, planned to advance on the Khalra-Barki axis, with 48 Infantry Brigade under Brigadier K. J. Shahaney, in the lead. One battalion of 65 Brigade (17 Rajput) was to secure Bedian to the South. The advance commenced in the early hours of 6 September, as planned. After some stiff fighting, the Brigade captured Hudiara drain area by the evening, although the enemy had blown up the bridge. A bailey bridge was constructed over the drain by the afternoon of 7 September under heavy enemy fire; and 65 Brigade under Brigadier LERB Ferris pushed through. 4 Sikh of this Brigade captured Barki in the early part of the night, after heavy hand to hand fighting. The bridge was, however, blown up by the enemy. The Central India Horse, the armoured regiment with the Division, played an important role in the advance. Its Commanding Officer Lieutenant Colonel S.C. Joshi was wounded and later succumbed to his injuries. In the Bedian area, which the enemy was holding with a battalion and some armour, the Rajputs could only secure up to the area East of the canal.

48 Brigade was ordered to capture Jahman but the attack failed. Brigadier Piara Singh replaced Brigadier Shahaney on 16 September. After this, another attack was launched and the village was captured.

4 Mountain Division Operations

Being a Mountain Division, this formation under Major General Gurbaksh Singh, was inadequately armed for plains warfare, particularly in artillery and recoilless guns. However, the Division had to be utilised, as there was no option and ad hoc arrangements made for necessary support The Divisional plan was as under:

(a) 62 Brigade under Brigadier H.C. Gahlaut was to advance on the Khemkaran-Kasur Road and capture the Rohi Nallah area and thereafter form a firm base to cover Khemkaran.

(b) Subsequently, 7 Brigade under Brigadier D.S. Sidhu was to secure the East bank of the Ichhogil Canal between Bedian and Ballanwala.

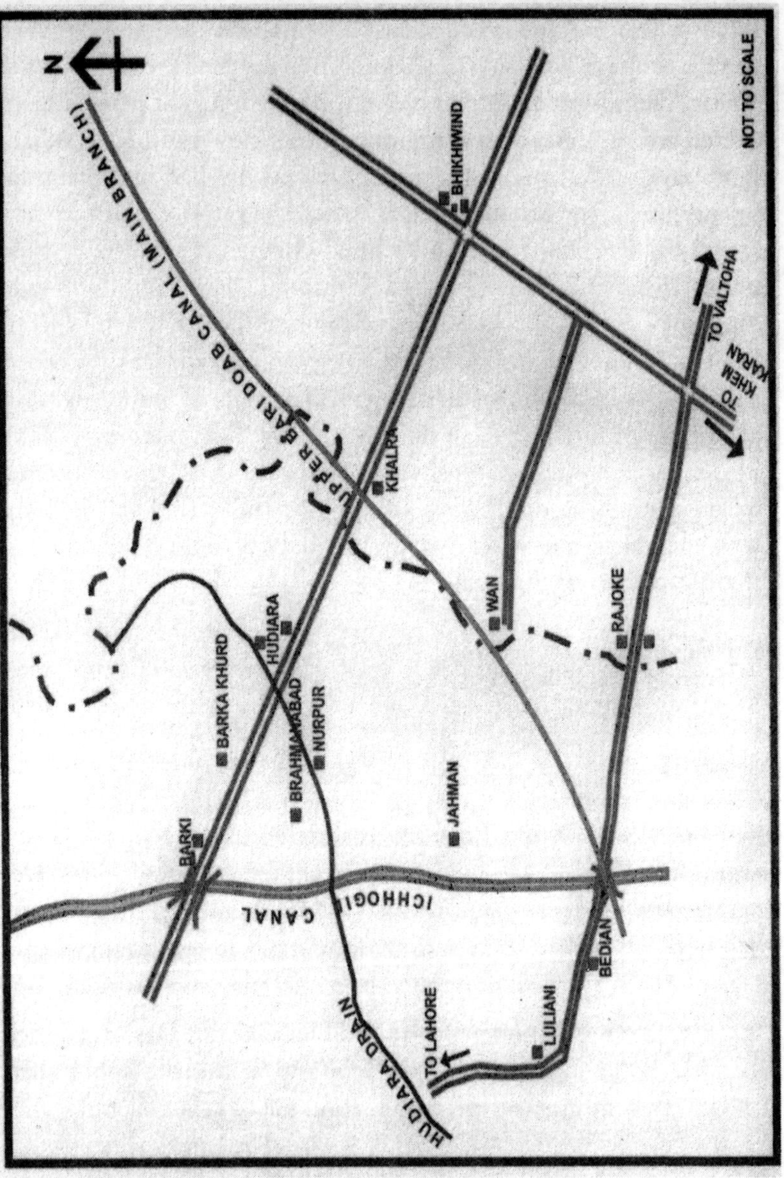

Map 5: 7 Infantry Division Operations

(c) Concurrently with (b) above, 62 Brigade was to secure the East bank of the Ichhogil canal between Ballanwala and Ganda Singh Wala.

(d) In the case of this Division, the bridges over the Ichhogil Canal were to be destroyed, to prevent a likely enemy counter offensive towards Khemkaran.

62 Brigade which had only arrived in the later part of the night 5/6 September, from the Simla Hills, commenced its advance in the early hours of the morning and secured its objectives, except the far Bund in the Rohi Nallah area by midday. 7 Brigade met with stiff opposition, and 4 Grenadiers secured the line of Ichhogil canal in the area of Thehpannun. 7 Grenadiers which was to take Ballanwala could not secure its objective, despite two attacks. The enemy shelled the entire area heavily and infiltrated a column of tanks and infantry through Ballanwala behind the forward troops in the early hours of 7 September. Some of the units withdrew from their position under this pressure, after having suffered heavy casualties.

Major General Gurbakhsh Singh at this stage appreciated that the enemy may launch his counter offensive in this area and decided to pull back to a defensive position in the rear and there hold the enemy. A few kilometres to the Northeast of Khemkaran was a suitable position around a place called Asal Uttar. This would cover the Khemkaran-Amritsar and Khemkaran-Patti axes; and lent itself to effective defence, as opposed to Khemkaran which could be bypassed. Under cover of heavy artillery fire and ably assisted by the Deccan Horse, under Lieutenant Colonel A.S. Vaidya, the remnants of the Division were withdrawn on 7 September. Fortunately, the enemy had not followed up for about twenty four hours; and the Division utilised the precious time to occupy its new defences. Lieutenant General Dhillon wanted the Divisional commander to be replaced. The Army Commander who visited the Asal Uttar position did not agree, but instead exhorted the Division to hold out in the new position. Subsequent events will show that Lieutenant

General Harbakhsh Singh's decision was fully vindicated by the Division.

It has been brought out earlier that Pakistan planned its counter offensive, with its strike force of 1 Armoured Division and 7 Infantry Division in an area well to the South of Kasur, most likely in the Abohar-Ganganagar area. However, as 7 Infantry Division was already committed, a significant change had to be made to her counter offensive plans. The Pakistani Commander-in-Chief, General Musa, ordered 11 Infantry Division to be grouped with 1 Armoured Division; and to launch the counter offensive through the Khemkaran area with a view to capture the Beas Bridge and isolate Amritsar. Major General Abdul Hamid, General Officer Commanding 11 Infantry Division was in overall command while 1 Armoured Division was commanded by Major General Nasir Ahmed Khan. The broad plan was that 11 Infantry Division with one of the three Armoured Brigades of the Armoured Division was to secure a lodgement in the Khemkaran area. Subsequently, the Armoured Division was to advance and secure the bridge at Harike, Jandiala Guru to the East of Amritsar and finally the bridge over the Beas, in quick succession. The advance was to commence on 8 September, after construction of a new bridge over the Ichhogil Canal, in place of an existing damaged bridge. Thus, about twenty-four hours were lost, in maintaining the momentum of the advance.

On the morning of 8 September, the Pakistani Armoured Division advanced forward and launched an attack on the Asal Uttar position along the Bhikhiwind axis with an Armoured Brigade. Although some positions of 1/9 Gorkha Rifles and 18 Rajputana Rifles were overrun, 62 and 7 Brigades supported by Deccan Horse and 3 Cavalry, were able to repulse the attacks, with some losses of tanks and personnel on both sides. However, enemy moves to outflank the position posed a serious threat. It was now clear that Pakistan was launching its main offensive in this sector. To meet the threat, therefore, 2 Independent Armoured Brigade under Brigadier Theograj, was placed under the command of 4 Mountain Division by 11 Corps. On the night of 8/9 September, the Pakistanis launched a second Armoured Brigade, this time, on the Patti axis. Units of 7 Brigade, supported by armour and artillery, again held out, despite repeated attacks by the enemy. In this attack, the Pakistanis suffered considerable tank losses. Brigadier Theograj now appreciated that the Pakistanis would try a wide outflanking move from the West, between Rohi Nallah and the Bhikhiwind road and deployed the better part of his Brigade to cover the area Lakhna-Mahmudpura-Chima. Further, a portion of the approaches were flooded so as to entice the enemy to the killing ground covered by the Centurion tanks of the Brigade.

As expected, the Pakistani Armoured Brigade attacked in the same area on 10 September and attempted to break through the position. First, they tried to overrun the 4 Grenadiers position. This Battalion held out with great determination and gallantry against heavy pressure by the enemy. In this action, Company Quartermaster Havildar Abdul Hameed was posthumously awarded the Param Vir Chakra for destroying three Patton tanks with his recoilless gun. However, the Centurion tanks had to rush to the help of the battalion. After this, the Pakistani Armoured Brigade attempted to break out of the position towards Mahmudpura. This was exactly what Brigadier Theograj wanted. His Centurion tanks destroyed a large number of the Pakistani Patton tanks and broke up the assault. In this action, the Pakistani Armoured Divisional Commander was wounded and his Artillery Brigade Commander Brigadier A.R. Shammi was killed in an ambush. His Armoured Brigade Commander expressed his inability to make any further progress, in view of the determined opposition that he encountered. The Pakistanis suffered considerable casualties, both in personnel and tanks. Despite this, on the morning of 11 September, Pakistan attempted an assault on the Patti axis, but this also failed. Later, the Commanding Officer of the Pakistani 4 Cavalry, Lieutenant Colonel Mahammad Nazir, with some of his personnel was captured, and his Brigade Operation Order (Headquarters 4 Armoured Brigade Operation Order Number 1 dated 8 September 1965) for the capture of Beas, was recovered from him. This order confirmed the Pakistani intention, without any doubt. The Pakistani plan for the capture of Beas, as it became apparent was on the following lines:

(a) 4 Armoured Brigade (4 Cavalry and 5 Horse, both Pattons) to advance along axis Valtoha-Patti-astride Sabraon Branch, to secure Rayya and the GT Road Bridge on the Beas.

(b) 3 Armoured Brigade (19 Lancers-Pattons) and 12 Cavalry (Chaffees) to advance along axis Khemkaran-Bhikkiwind-astride Kasur Branch to secure Jandiala Guru.

(c) 5 Armoured Brigade (24 Cavalry-Pattons) to advance along axis Khemkaran-Bhikkiwind to provide left flank protection and to cut the rear of 7 Infantry Division.

Despite repeated efforts to break through the Indian position at Asal Uttar, the Pakistanis were unable to make any headway and suffered tremendous losses. A total of 97 tanks were lost by Pakistan. A number of tanks in good running condition were captured by the Indian Army. Having lost the ability to continue the offensive any further, the Pakistani Commander-in-Chief called off the offensive and pulled out the remnants of his 1 Armoured Division towards the North, to meet the developing threat from the Indian 1 Corps. The Indian 4 Mountain Division and 2 Independent Armoured Brigade thus frustrated the Pakistani major offensive and did the Indian Army proud. Not only the Infantry and Armour, but the Artillery and Engineers also played a significant role in the destruction of the enemy. Thus came to an ignominious end Ayub's boast that his tanks "would reach New Delhi along the Grand Trunk Road in a matter of hours".

Later, in his book, "My Version", the Pakistani Commander-in-Chief General Musa revealed that the aim of the major offensive was to capture Amritsar. He states that he had given sufficient time (more than 10 days or so before the start of the War on 6 September) to the formation commanders to plan the operation, which was not a difficult or complicated one as no crossing of any major water obstacle was involved and as the enemy (4 Mountain Division) was disorganised. He states that leading elements of 4 Armoured Brigade

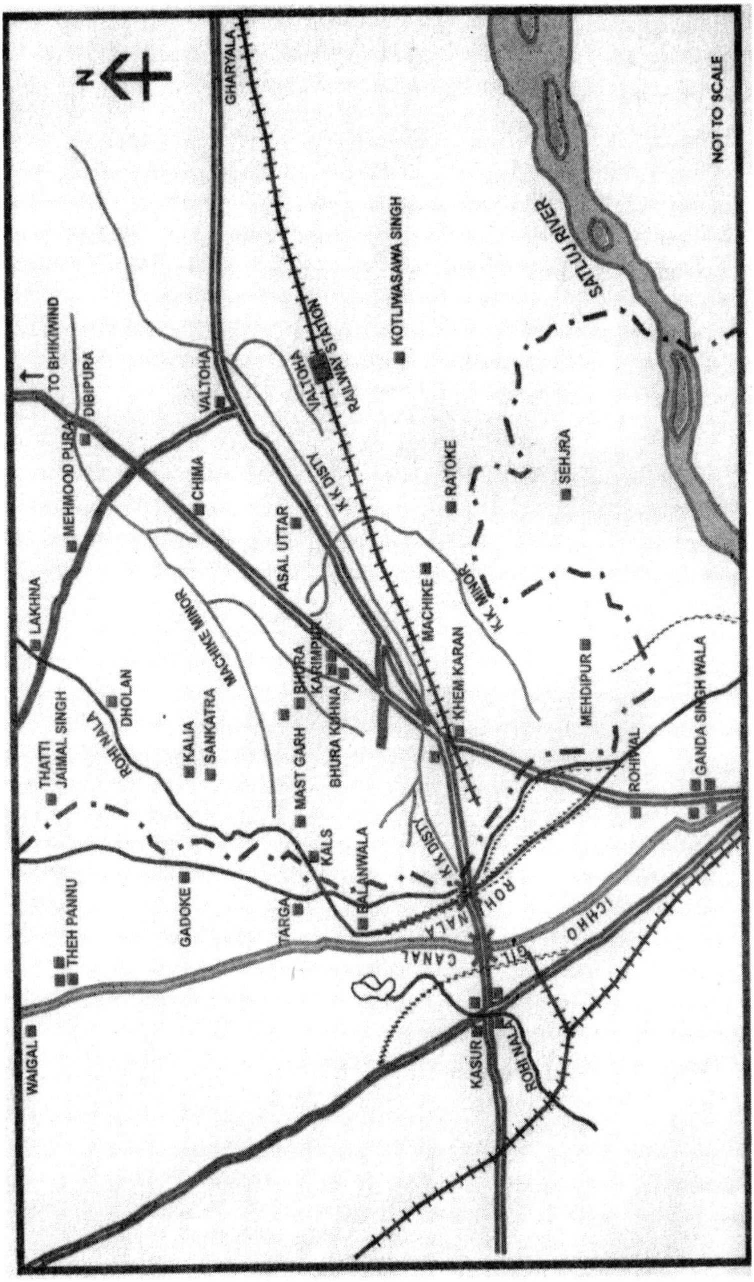

Map 6: Asal Uttar - Khemkaran

initially pressed forward with determination and secured their objective but the rest of the Brigade, particularly the Motor Battalion, could not fetch up. In the case of 5 Armoured Brigade, it had reached Valtoha but the Brigade Commander withdrew to Khemkaran, due to some confusion. He attributes the failure of the offensive to ineffective leadership in the higher echelons of command. He reveals that he had to call off the offensive due to heavy tank losses, failure of command set up, stiffness of enemy resistance and loss of ability to pursue with the offensive any further.

After the withdrawal of the bulk of the Pakistani armour. 4 Mountain Division was ordered to retake Khemkaran. Gurbakhsh Singh used 7 Brigade for the purpose. Two new battalions, namely 4 Sikh and 2 Mahar were given to 7 Brigade for the operation. 4 Sikh were used on an outflanking movement, while 2 Mahar were ordered to put in a frontal attack on the Khemkaran Distributory position. The operation was launched on 12 September but unfortunately about two companies of 4 Sikh were captured by the enemy; while 2 Mahar, supported by Deccan Horse, could not overcome the position despite some initial success and suffering heavy casualties. A second attack was put in by 7 Brigade but this also failed. Subsequently, 4 Division was given two new brigades, namely 29 Brigade and 41 Brigade, but lost 7 Brigade. The Division launched yet another attack on Khemkaran on 21 September but even this could not make any headway. It was discovered that the enemy determinedly held the position with a strong Brigade group with armour support.

In the Fazilka area, 67 Infantry Brigade under Brig Bant Singh was responsible for the sector from Fazilka to Ganganagar. The Pakistanis attacked opposite Suleimanki a number of times but could only succeed in capturing some outposts. They could not penetrate the main defences despite repeated efforts.

23 Mountain Division was brought forward from the East during the later stages of the operations. It was planned that this Division should advance on the axis Derababa Nanak-Narowal-Pasrur, after

26 September. However, the Division was not actually used as the war ended earlier.

OPERATIONS IN THE SIALKOT SECTOR

1 Corps of Indian Army, a newly raised formation under Lieutenant General P.O. Dunn, was given the task of isolating Sialkot from Lahore by driving a wedge into the area of Daska, North of Gujranwala. The Corps had one Armoured Division, two Infantry Divisions and one Mountain Division, under its command. The Corps plan broadly was as under:

(a) 26 Infantry Division under Major General M.L. Thapan was to secure Anula and Bajragarhi by first light, 8 September.

(b) 6 Mountain Division under Major General S.K. Korla was to secure Maharajke and Charwa by first light, 8 September.

(c) 14 Infantry Division under Major General R.K Ranjit Singh was to capture Zaffarwal on 8 September.

(d) 1 Armoured Division under Major General Rajindar Singh was to advance in the early hours of 8 September and capture Phillora and Pagwal by last light the same day.

Subsequently, the Armoured Division was to advance to Chawinda, and thereafter on relief by 14 Infantry Division, was to advance further South, for which detailed planning was to be done later.

The finalisation of the Indian offensive plan took time as two schools of thought had emerged on the choice of the area of operations. Lieutenant General Harbaksh Singh advocated an offensive into the Sialkot sector via the Indian enclaves of Nainakot and Narot involving a crossing of the Ravi. His reasons were:

(a) The chances of surprise were better as a concentration of troops in the Gurdaspur area might be construed as a part of the forces assembled for employment in the Lahore Sector.

On the other hand, a large scale concentration of troops in Samba area was liable to be detected especially as the only road from Madhopur to Samba was under observation from within Pakistani territory.

(b) The concentration of troops in the Gurdaspur area would take less time due to availability of rail and road facilities and shorter distance.

(c) An offensive from the Gurdaspur direction would take the Pakistanis in the Sialkot sector from a flank and threaten their rear, deployed along the Jammu border.

(d) The existing administrative set up and communications were better to meet logistic requirements of the forces operating from the Gurdaspur area.

(e) The initial crossing of the Ravi would not face a serious problem as use would be made of the Indian enclaves across the Ravi as bridgeheads. It was considered that Pakistan would not pre-empt this by occupying these enclaves as she had been anxious to confine the fighting to Jammu & Kashmir territory scrupulously.

(f) It was felt that a concentration of forces in Samba area would take longer, especially as the large fleet of tanks would have to be ferried over long distances on the limited number of tank transporters. This would forewarn the Pakistanis of the direction and timing of attack thus obviating surprise. It would give them extra time to face any attack from this direction.

(g) An offensive from Samba direction would not permit mutual support between 11 and 1 Corps especially as the Ravi would not permit quick switching of forces between the two Corps. (This aspect came to the fore during the crisis of the Asal Uttar battle.)

(h) Indian forces would be operating on exterior lines on either side of the Ravi, while the Pakistanis could switch forces quickly between Lahore and Sialkot sectors using interior lines and better rail and road communication networks.

General Chaudhuri preferred an offensive along Samba-Ramgarh direction for the following reasons:

(a) The terrain in the Sialkot Sector was good tank country where 1 Armoured Division could produce better results by advancing along the grain of the country.

(b) An offensive in this sector would pick up momentum from the very beginning. The area was wide enough to permit manoeuvre to the armoured division and there were no major obstacles to be crossed until the Marala-Ravi Link Canal (MRLC).

(c) Operations in this sector would have a direct and close influence on Pakistani operations in the neighbouring sectors of Akhnoor and Naushahra. In case of an Indian offensive in the Sialkot Sector, Pakistan would be forced to move troops for its defence by pulling troops out of Jammu & Kashmir, thus reducing her offensive potential there.

(d) An offensive in this Sector would automatically give added depth and security to the vital life-line linking Pathankot with Jammu and Srinagar.

(e) India would augment her military potential by integrating the considerable assets of 26 Infantry Division located at Jammu.

(f) It was felt that a river crossing, especially in the monsoon period, would be a risky operation as there were no bridges over the Ravi linking Gurdaspur with the Indian enclaves in the area. In addition, an advance from Gurdaspur direction would be against the grain of the country, thus involving crossings over a number of sandy nalas.

Considering the various aspects, General Chaudhuri had decided, by the middle of August that the 1 Corps offensive would be launched into the Sialkot Sector from the Samba direction. The area between the Degh Nadi and the Aik Nala east of Sialkot, with a frontage of over 20 kilometres, was selected for an offensive thrust by 1 Corps. The plan was to launch a simultaneous attack by I and 11 Corps in the Sialkot and Lahore Sectors respectively. While Lahore was the most prestigious objective in Pakistan, Sialkot town was a close second. The plan was, however, not aimed at a direct capture of either due to the fears of heavy casualties in fighting in a built-up area. In the Sialkot Sector, the security of Pathankot-Jammu road and the MRLC were vital to the respective opponents and their plans were, to a degree, oriented to that purpose.

Sialkot is the most important town and a nodal point of communications in this sector. It was linked to Chhamb by the Marala road bridge over the Chenab. Zafarwal, on the east bank of the Degh, was another nodal point linked to Sialkot, Pasrur, Chawinda and Narowal. The following important west-east laterals radiated from Sialkot:

(a) Sialkot-Bajragahi-Maharajke-Charwa-Nakhnal. This track ran just south and parallel to the international border.

(b) Sialkot-Phillora-Zafarwal

(c) Sialkot-Badiana-Chawinda-Zafarwal

(d) Sialkot-Badiana-Pasrur-Narowal was a good road.

The Sialkot-Narowal railway ran between (b) and (c). The area was densely populated and a large number of villages existed along the tracks especially where the north-south tracks intersected with the west-east laterals.

Important roads and tracks leading into the area from the Indian border were as under:

(a) Jammu-Sialkot road with Jammu about 28 kilometres from the border and Sialkot 12 kilometres. A road links Sialkot to Wazirabad on the Pakistan National Highway, Lahore-Peshawar.

(b) Maharajke-Pagowal-Badiana. It crossed the Sialkot-Phillora track and the Sialkot-Narowal railway line. Badiana was linked to Sialkot, Pasrur and Chawinda.

(c) Charwa-Sabzpir-Phillora-Chawinda-Pasrur. This track ran in the centre of 1 Corps area of operations and was the shortest approach from Samba to the important town and communication centre of Pasrur. Chawinda was an important nodal point on this approach. It lay at the apex of the triangle Chawinda-Badiana-Pasrur which blocked any direct approach to the MRLC through the central sector an- checked any outflanking move from Zafarwal side to threaten the rear of the troops deployed against any Indian offensive from Jammu-Samba direction. After securing a segment of the MRLC, a thrust could be launched to cut the Pakistan National Highway in Wazirabad area with dire consequences to the security of Pakistan.

(d) Nakhnal-Rangre-Tharoh-Dugri. The track ran along the western bank of the Degh nadi and cut the Maharajke-Sabzpir-Rangre-Zafarwal lateral at Rangre while cutting the Chawinda-Zafarwal lateral at Dugri. Tharoh-Dugri area could be a base for outflanking Chawinda defences.

The terrain in this sector is flat with tall crops obstructing long distance observation. The villages are identifiable by the small groves of trees around them. Pakistan had not improved the tracks on its side of the border to hinder large scale vehicular movement. The condition of roads on the Indian side was better but near the border these had not been developed to undertake heavy traffic. Aik Nala runs inside Indian territory north of Charwa-Bajragarhi track, turning south into Pakistan territory between Sialkot and Bajragarhi. Aik and Degh nalas could be crossed in dry season at suitable crossing places.

Both India and Pakistan had assessed the military significance of Lahore and Sialkot Sectors in their offensive and defensive strategy. It was clear that both sides lacked the capability for major offensive operations in more than one area. Considering the time constraints of a short duration war, it was obvious that the main offensive would be based on their respective armoured divisions for victory or at least for the capture of large tracts of important land. While Pakistan chose the Khem Karan Sector, India's choice fell on Sialkot Sector for their major armour thrusts. India planned an offensive-defensive strategy to capture and secure territory up to the Ichhogil Canal in the Lahore Sector while launching her main offensive in the Sialkot Sector. Pakistan on the other hand, planned a defensive posture in Sialkot Sector intending to lose as little territory as possible in her secondary area of operations in the Sialkot area while opting for the kill in the Amritsar Sector.

India had considered a Pakistani offensive in the Khem Karan area likely. Similarly Pakistan had assessed an Indian offensive in Sialkot Sector and had studied the defence strategy for this Sector as a Staff College exercise. Pakistan's concept was that India would launch a three-pronged attack along the DBN-Narowal, Ramgarh-Pasrur and Jammu-Sialkot axes; initially exerting pressure against DBN and Sialkot to suck in maximum forces to these flanks. Thereafter India would launch her major thrust in the soft central sector. They felt that such an operation would enable India to destroy Pak forces in piecemeal battles of attrition. The MRLC was farther from the border than the Ichhogil Canal, leaving unprotected a large tract of terrain including the important towns of Sialkot, Badiana and Pasrur. Pakistan, keeping the MRLC as a last ditch battle line, decided to defend the important towns and communication centres of Sialkot, Chawinda and Narowal to lessen her territorial loss. Pakistan planned to stop the Indian offensive as far forward as possible, ahead of the MRLC while employing fire and manoeuvre as the doctrine of defence to cause maximum attrition on the attacker. Sialkot was to be the pivot of defence. The composition of the brigades varied according to the visualisation of the Indian threat and the tactical importance of the defended area. Due to the distances involved, the defended areas were not mutually supporting. The Chawinda-Badiana-Pasrur triangle was central to the defence structure of the defence plan. Considering the various factors,

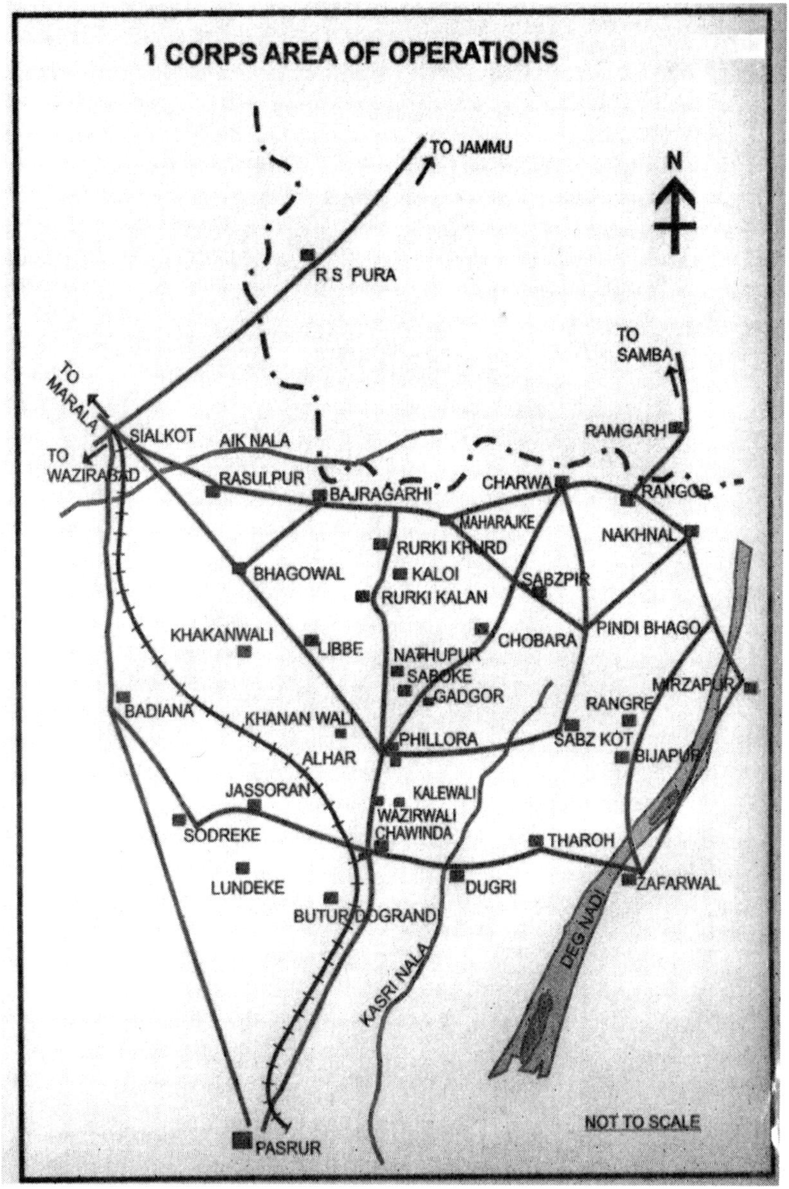

Map 7: 1 Corps Area of Operations

15 Pakistan Division planned to hold the line Jassar-Narowal-Chawinda-Sialkot as under:

(a) 101 Infantry Brigade (Two infantry battalions and two Sherman regiments)—Sialkot Sector

(b) 24 Infantry Brigade (Two infantry battalions and 25 Cavalry equipped with Pattons—Chawinda Sector

(c) 115 Infantry Brigade (Two infantry battalions and one Sherman regiment)—Jassar-Narowal Sector

(d) 104 Infantry Brigade (One infantry battalion and one Sherman regiment)—Behind Sialkot as reserve

6 Armoured Division was in Daska area as the GHQ reserve. The raising of this division was not complete when the war started. Two of its armoured regiments (11 Cavalry and 13 Lancers) had been committed for operations in the Akhnoor Sector.

The above pattern of deployment indicates that Pakistan had intended to hold the two extremities at Jassar and Sialkot close to the border, using the defence potential of the Ravi and the built up area respectively, while her defences in the centre were further back from the border. Pakistan had, of course, planned to maintain her presence in the Central Sector along the border with Charwa and Maharajke acting as strong points. Pakistan had located Rangers, Mujahids and armed ex-servicemen in these villages, each reinforced by about an infantry company with elements of the Recce & Support battalion as the Indian threat became imminent. The idea was to gain early and reliable information about the direction and strength of the Indian attack in addition to delaying the advance. The plan of 24 Pakistan Brigade was to deploy an infantry battalion in prepared defences in Gadgor area in a delaying role with the rest of the brigade in the main defences at Chawinda. 15 Pakistan Division had moved into its battle locations by first light on 6 September. No mines were laid by the Pakistanis in this sector; perhaps they wanted the area free of mines for the operation of their armoured division or it might have been due to shortage of mines.

On the Indian side, General Chaudhuri had planned to launch his strongest Corps (1 Armoured Division, 6 Mountain Division, 14 Infantry Division and 26 Infantry Division) in the Sialkot Sector. The Indian Army had appreciated that the Pakistani main defence line would be along the Sialkot-Badiana-Pasrur road with a covering position at Chawinda. An infantry battalion was expected to hold Maharajke and Charwa as strong points with about a strong company each, with delaying positions between the border and Chawinda. The essential ingredients of the Indian plan were surprise and relentless offensive action. The plan revolved around 1 Armoured Division as the prima donna while the infantry formations had secondary and supporting roles. The armoured division was tasked to launch a deep, vigorous and paralysing thrust into the guts of enemy defences and dominate the battlefield thereafter, using its fire potential, offensive action and mobility. General Chaudhuri chose Lieutenant General P.O. Dunn to command 1 Corps.

Dunn, an infantry officer, had neither served in any armoured formation nor had he been exposed to any active operational command assignment since the end of World War II. He had earlier been recalled from leave pending retirement to command an adhoc force in the Rann of Kutch. The fighting in the Rann ended before Dunn could contribute much. During 'Op Ablaze', General Chaudhuri got Government sanction for Dunn's promotion and appointment to command 1 Corps on the plea that he was the best general, in the Indian Army's moment of destiny, to command the offensive by 1 Corps. It involved supersession's including that of Major General R.S Sparrow, MVC, GOC I Armoured Division, who agreed to serve under Dunn. General Chaudhuri had chosen the commander and area of operations for his strongest corps with high expectations in the forthcoming war.

Operations were launched on the night of 7/8 September generally as planned, but as 14 Division could not complete its concentration till 8 September, two of its available brigades were parcelled out to other formations. Thus, 35 Infantry Brigade was allotted to 6 Mountain Division and 15 Infantry Brigade to the

Armoured Division. 26 Infantry Division and 6 Mountain Division captured their objectives in time, without much difficulty.

1 Armoured Division Operations

1 Armoured Division had two Brigades, namely, 1 Armoured Brigade under Brigadier K.K. Singh and 43 Lorried Infantry Brigade under Brigadier H.S. Dhillon. The Divisional plan envisaged an advance on a two-brigade front:

(a) 1 Armoured Brigade on the axis Ramgarh-Hathbal-Sabzkot-Chobara-Phillora.

(b) 43 Lorried Infantry Brigade on axis Deoli-Salarian-Saidanwali-Cross Roads-Mastpur-Salowal-BhajowaI.

1 Armoured Brigade set out at 0600 hours on 8 September, as planned and reached the enemy screen in the area Pindi-Bhago-Narsingh-Chobara, which was overcome after some fighting. 43 Lorried Brigade, having had to change its axis of advance due to rain having made the original route slushy and impassable, turned back and advanced via Ramgarh in the early hours of 8 September. The Brigade cleared Salarian and captured Cross Roads. Subsequently, the Brigade was ordered to advance via Maharajke-Kaloi and capture PagowaI. Advancing on the morning of 9 September, the Brigade secured Kaloi but could not get to PagowaI. Heavy enemy shelling and air attacks throughout 10 September followed by heavy rain made all tracks unfit. However, on the morning of 11 September, 1 Armoured Brigade advanced through Rurki Khurd-Rurki Kalan towards Phillora. The enemy had two regiments of armour and some infantry in the Phillora area. As 1 Armoured Brigade reached the line Libbe-Nathupur-Saboke, there was a serious clash with the Pakistani armour. 4 Horse, by an outflanking movement, compelled the enemy to withdraw from the Eastern side. 43 Lorried Brigade then tried to launch an attack on the Phillora position, but due to enemy's heavy artillery fire and strafing, could not press on. The Brigade then cleared the villages Khananwali and Wachuke. Thereafter, Phillora Cross Roads was

secured by 1530 hours on 11 September. 17 Horse supported the operation throughout with great gallantry and aggressiveness. After the capture of Phillora, the enemy tried to dislodge the Brigade but could not succeed. It also transpired that the Commander of the 15 Infantry Division, who was trying to land in the Phillora area by helicopter was shot up by 17 Horse and killed.

Attempts to capture Pagowal with 62 Cavalry on September 11, could not succeed. Subsequently, the task was given to 6 Mountain Division. 69 Brigade of this Division under Brigadier E.A. Vas, supported by 62 Cavalry, took this position on 13 September against heavy opposition. Later the Pakistanis counter attacked but were beaten back.

Plans were now made for the capture of Chawinda by the Armoured Division. Briefly, the plan was that 4 Horse was to advance from Chahar and cut the Badiana-Pasrur and Chawinda-Pasrur roads in the area of the Railway line Sialkot-Narowal. Thereafter, 17 Horse was to advance to Alhar from Gil and then swing towards Kalewali-Chawinda. 16 Cavalry and 2 Lancers were to provide flank protection from the West and the East. Once the armour had created a favourable situation, 43 Lorried Brigade was to attack Chawinda. The operation was to take place on 14 September.

Area Chawinda was held by about two regiments of armour and infantry. 1 Armoured Brigade launched its operation on 14 September but, due to stiff opposition, could only secure some of the objectives, namely, Wazirwali and Alhar Railway Station. Kalewali was secured by 5 JAT but was recaptured by enemy armour. However, in the early hours of 15 September, Kalewali was again recaptured by 5 JAT.

Owing to the heavy opposition encountered at Chawinda, the General Officer Commanding 1 Corps decided that unless a strong force was established behind Chawinda and the position cut off, it would not be possible to capture the town. Thus, 17 Horse and 8 Garhwal Rifles group was ordered to establish itself in the area Jassoran-Butur Dograndi area on 16 September. On the morning of

16 September, 17 Horse with a company of 9 Dogra captured Jassoran, after suffering heavy losses. 8 Garhwal Rifles managed to reach Butur Dograndi after suffering heavy casualties, including the loss of their Commanding officer Lieutenant Colonel J.E. Jhirad. However, Butur Dograndi changed hands several times, with the enemy ultimately retaking part of the position. 43 Lorried Brigade was then ordered to launch their attack on Chawinda on 17 September. However, as the troops were far back and could not fetch up, the attack was called off. During the heavy tank battles, Lieutenant Colonel A.B. Tarapore of 17 Horse was killed. He led his regiment with great distinction and gallantry and inflicted considerable tank losses on the enemy. He was posthumously awarded the Param Vir Chakra.

6 Mountain Division Operations

Chawinda position proved to be a tough nut to crack. The Corps Commander decided to put in an attack with 6 Mountain Division with armour in support. For this purpose, 6 Division received two Brigades of 14 Division, namely 35 Brigade and 58 Brigade. The attack was to go in the early hours of 18 September but had to be postponed to facilitate adequate reconnaissance. In the meantime, Jassoran and Butur Dograndi were lost, despite determined resistance and heavy losses among the Garhwalis. However, 20 Rajput from 43 Lorried Brigade recaptured the position at night 18/19 September.

Major General S.K. Korla planned to attack the Chawinda position with two brigades up, after considerable softening of the enemy defences by the Indian Air Force and artillery. The attack was launched during the night 19/20 September. Due to heavy counter bombardment as well as fire against infantry, the attack could not be pressed home. The enemy air was also very active. The attacking troops suffered heavy casualties due to tank and artillery fire and air attacks. Chawinda, therefore, remained elusive.

In all these operations, 1 Corps captured about 490 square kilometres of enemy territory and inflicted heavy tank losses on the enemy (captured 11, knocked out 133 and subsequently destroyed 31). 693 of the enemy were killed, as against 575 lost by the Corps. 138 prisoners were taken. However, a large number of personnel in the Corps were wounded.

Chhamb-Akhnoor Sector

Consequent to the major offensive by the Indian Army in Punjab, the Pakistanis started thinning out their troops from the Chhamb-Akhnoor Sector. 10 Infantry Division was, therefore, ordered to recapture the lost territory. A divisional attack was launched on 9/10 September on the position covering Jaurian, but could not succeed. It was found that while the enemy had withdrawn most of his armour, sufficient infantry was left behind in well-prepared defences. The Pakistanis in the meantime infiltrated into the Kalidhar Range, with a view to cutting off the Akhnoor-Nowshera Road. 191 Brigade was moved to the North to deal with the threat. This Brigade managed to clear most of the enemy from the Kalidhar Range.

OPERATIONS IN RAJASTHAN

Southern Command under Lieutenant General Moti Sagar had the task of tying down the enemy forces in the Sind area. 11 Infantry Division under Major General N.C. Rawlley, was responsible for operations in this area.

The Division had a very large front to cover in the Thar desert. In this area, as troop deployment was very thin on the ground, both sides were able to make some limited gains. In the Barmer Sector, 30 Infantry Brigade of 11 Division captured Gadra on 8 September and cleared the bulk of the bulge, of the enemy. Subsequently, the Pakistani 51 Infantry Brigade captured Munabao Railway Station. On 19 September, 11 Division captured Dali and certain other posts.

In the Jaisalmer Sector, some enemy posts were captured by 11 Division. The Pakistanis in turn captured the old Fort of Kishangarh.

CEASEFIRE AND TASHKENT AGREEMENT

The Secretary General of the United Nations, U. Thant, had been endeavouring ever since the Pakistani infiltration started into Jammu and Kashmir on 5 August, to bring the fighting to an end and to have the Ceasefire Line respected by both sides. In his Report to the Security Council on 3 September, he stated that on the advice of General Nimmo, the Chief Military Observer, he summoned the representatives of both sides separately. He asked the Pakistani representative to convey to his Government, his "very serious concern about the situation that was developing in Kashmir, involving the crossing of the CFL from the Pakistan side by numbers of armed men and their attacks on military positions on the Indian side of the line, and also his strong appeal that the CFL be observed". He asked the Indian representative to convey to his Government, "my urgent appeal for restraint as regards any retaliatory action from their side". Subsequently, the Secretary General reported that he was unable to get necessary assurance from Pakistan, but received an assurance from the Indian representative that India would act with restraint and respect the CFL, if Pakistan did so. He indicated in his Report that if a summary of CFL infractions was published, it would clearly put the blame on Pakistan. On 1 September, the Secretary General publicly appealed for peace. Presidents Nasser of UAR and Tito of Yugoslavia also appealed for a ceasefire on 3 September. All the elected Members of the Security Council appealed for a ceasefire on 4 September. On 8 September, the Security Council called for withdrawal of all the armed personnel back to the positions held by them before 5 August. It may be mentioned that it was the first time that the United States and Soviet Union voted together on such an important issue affecting war and peace.

The Indian representative, G. Parthasarathy, explained that the Kashmir issue remained alive because the Security Council refused to face the fact of aggression by Pakistan and clarified that the political status of Kashmir was not negotiable. The Indian Prime Minister wanted certain essential pre-conditions to be fulfilled for a ceasefire, namely, acceptable guarantees from Pakistan that all infiltrators and military personnel would be withdrawn from Indian Kashmir and that no further attacks will be made. He clarified that "we cannot go from one cease fire to another without our being satisfied that Pakistan will not repeat its acts of violation and aggression in the future". On the other hand, President Ayub Khan contended that the so-called freedom fighters were not raiders but sons of the soil and harped on non-implementation of the UN Resolution (on Plebiscite) in Kashmir!

U. Thant made personal visits to Rawalpindi and New Delhi during the period 9-12 September, in his efforts to bring about a ceasefire. The Pakistan Government, having accepted that her forces had crossed into Indian territory, announced that for a ceasefire, she wanted certain conditions to be fulfilled, These were, the complete withdrawal of all Indian and Pakistani forces from Kashmir, establishment of a United Nation's force drawn from the Afro-Asian Nations to maintain security in the State pending a plebiscite, and a plebiscite to be held within three months. To this, Prime Minister Shastri stated that "not one of these conditions is acceptable to India". He said that "Pakistan talks glibly of a plebiscite in Kashmir while it is not prepared to have a free election in its own country. How would Pakistan like a plebiscite in the Pakhtoon area to find out whether it wishes to remain a part of Pakistan? How would Pakistan like a plebiscite in East Bengal to find out whether the people of East Bengal want to be ruled from Rawalpindi?" India was, however, prepared to accept an unconditional ceasefire which would restore the status-quo-ante. The Secretary General found the Indian attitude to be more amenable. U. Thant wrote to both sides, suggesting a cease fire at 1830 hours on 14 September. India requested for an extension of the time by 24 hours and accepted the proposal. However, Prime Minister Shastri stated that the ceasefire would apply to uniformed soldiers and that India would be free to deal with the infiltrators who were still within her territory. Pakistan, in its reply, continued to harp on her three-point demand. As the Secretary General could not accept any pre-condition from either side, the truce could not be achieved. Prime Minister Shastri told the Parliament on 16 September that in the talks with U. Thant, "India made it clear that we were fully determined to maintain the sovereignty and territorial integrity of India of which the State of Jammu and Kashmir was an integral part. From this resolve we could never be deflected, no matter what the pressure or the threat. These were not conditions attached to our acceptance of the ceasefire, but were meant to be a clear and unequivocal reiteration of our stand in regard to these matters."

During this period, the Chinese tried to put pressure on India. On 8 September, a formal note was sent to India, accusing her of violating the Sikkim border and to halt provocations. Their statement accusing India of aggression said, "Indian aggression against anyone of its neighbours concerns all of its neighbours." Again on 17 September, China accused India of maintaining 56 military installations on the Tibetan side of the Sikkim-Tibetan border and demanded their dismantling. Otherwise, they warned that, "Indian Government must bear responsibility for all the grave consequences arising therefrom". They also said that thirteen representations to the Indian Government about 300 incursions into the Chinese territory had been ignored; and demanded return of four Tibetans, 800 sheep and 59 yaks allegedly abducted from Tibet. India in its reply, stated that strict instructions against any border transgressions were issued to the Indian Army and that these were fully observed. India also conveyed that it would accept joint inspection of the border facilities. Expressing the hope that China would not take advantage of the situation, Shastri told the House, "the might of China will not deter us from defending our territorial integrity." Subsequently, it was learnt that the Americans administered a strong warning to China, "to stay out of the Indo-Pakistan Conflict".

U. Thant suggested to the Security Council on 16 September to invoke Chapter VII of the United Nations Charter, permitting the Council to use military and economic force, if necessary, to ensure an end to the fighting. Apparently, U. Thant felt that considerable pressure was necessary to obtain compliance of Pakistan to the ceasefire resolution. However, the Council did not agree to this. On 20 September, the Security Council adopted a third resolution, demanding a ceasefire on the morning of 22 September and subsequent withdrawal of all armed personnel to the positions held on 5 August. The Council also expressed willingness to consider the steps to be taken to assist towards a settlement of the political problem. Concurrently, the Council called on all States to refrain from any action which might aggravate the situation in the area. This was obviously a warning to China. India accepted the ceasefire but made it clear that it did not accept proposals regarding political settlement. Bhutto, the Pakistani Foreign Minister, threatened in the Security Council, "we will wage a war for thousand years"; but in the end accepted the ceasefire. He warned that Pakistan would withdraw from the international organisation, if the Security Council does not exert its full force "behind an equitable and honourable settlement of the Jammu and Kashmir dispute".

Quite obviously, at this point of time, the military situation compelled Pakistan to accept the ceasefire and restoration of status quo ante. After the serious reverse in the battles in the Khemkaran and Chawinda areas and the considerable attrition that she suffered of her military might, Pakistan had no option, but to accept the UN Resolution. It has also to be remembered that military and economic assistance to both countries had been stopped since the beginning of the hostilities. Thus, at 0330 hours on 23 September (Indian Standard Time) the ceasefire came into effect. As for the Chinese, on 22 September, they announced that the Indians had complied with their demands for dismantling the disputed military structures.

After the ceasefire came into effect on 23 September, both sides started consolidating existing positions, which is, of course, understandable in the initial stages. However, Pakistan committed certain serious violations across the line, obviously with a view to capturing as much territory as possible, to compensate for the territory that she had lost in Punjab, so that at the negotiating table later, she would not be in a disadvantageous position. On the night of 23/24 September, Pakistani troops launched a battalion attack with tanks. In the Fazilka area in the Rajasthan desert which was held thinly by the Indians, the Pakistanis launched several attacks and captured a large amount of territory (most of the 4,100 square kilometres which she claimed). This was corroborated, not only by intercepts of Pakistani signals directing their troops to capture maximum possible territory, but also by physical observation by United Nations observers on 13 November, when they saw Pakistani tanks in action. In Jammu and Kashmir also, Pakistanis continued with infiltration, raids, artillery fire and even battalion-sized attacks in many areas across the cease fire line, forcing India to take defensive measures. Apart from all these, a large number of infiltrators continued to operate inside Jammu and Kashmir, in certain pockets. The Security Council took serious note of these violations and called for strict observance of the ceasefire and for restoration of status-quo-ante. It was, however, clear that unless something concrete was done, the ceasefire may not hold.

Earlier, while the ceasefire negotiations were going on, on 19 September, the Soviet Union had invited India and Pakistan to meet in Soviet Union for discussions. Again, on 21 November, the Soviet Union renewed her suggestion for such a meeting at Tashkent. This move was also supported by the United States. Both sides accepted the invitation and a summit Conference opened on 4 January 1966 between Shastri and Ayub. The Soviet Prime Minister Kosygin initially wanted the two leaders to hold bilateral discussions and stated that he would only come into the picture if his help was required by the parties concerned. At the outset, both sides adopted firm attitudes, in support of their postures. Ayub insisted on a political settlement of Kashmir. Shastri declined to negotiate on the political future of Kashmir, but wanted a No-War Agreement. Pakistan reiterated that such an Agreement was not possible without settling the fundamental issue of Kashmir. India reiterated that while she was prepared to talk about any subject, including Kashmir, there was no question of negotiating its future. As the Conference appeared to get bogged down, Kosygin stepped in and used all the diplomatic skills under his command over a period of time, to get the two leaders to agree for implementation of the ceasefire proposals and arrive on a basis for further bilateral discussions on the various issues involved.

Ultimately, an Agreement, known as the "Tashkent Declaration" was signed on 10 January 1966. The Declaration envisaged "all armed personnel of the two countries shall be withdrawn not later than 25 February 1966 to the positions they held prior to 5 August 1965, and both sides shall observe the ceasefire terms on the Ceasefire Line". Prisoners of war were to be repatriated promptly. Normal diplomatic relations were to be re-established and measures for restoring economic and cultural relations were to be discussed. Both sides agreed to continue meetings at the highest and at other levels on matters of direct concern to both countries. Both recognised the need to set up joint India-Pakistan bodies. Both the leaders agreed to abandon the use of force and to base their relations "on the principles of non-interference in the internal affairs of each other". They also agreed, "to create good neighbourly relations between India and Pakistan in accordance with the UN Charter. The Declaration further said, "they consider that the interests of peace in their region and particularly in the Indo-Pakistani Sub-continent and, indeed the interests of the peoples of India and Pakistan, were not served by the continuance of tensions between the two countries". It was against this background that Jammu and Kashmir was discussed, and each of the sides set forth its respective position.

In the early hours of 11 January Prime Minister Shastri died of a heart attack, in Tashkent. He was succeeded as Prime Minister, by Mrs. Indira Gandhi, in a smooth change over. Though diminutive in height and perhaps unimpressive to the Pakistanis, Shastri proved to be a sagacious statesman and a courageous leader, who served his country with credit.

Soon after the Tashkent Agreement, the military commanders of both sides met and resolved among themselves the various problems concerning the implementation. Disengagement of troops was completed by 30 January and withdrawal of all forces to pre-war positions had been completed by 25 February.

ADMINISTRATION AND LOGISTICS

Administration is the life blood of war and is central to the success or failure of a campaign. After nearly three weeks of high intensity fighting, the Indo-Pak conflict was slipping into a war of attrition in which considerations of logistical sustainability tended to come increasingly to the fore.

Due to indigenisation, India had achieved a degree of sufficiency in its requirements of small arms, munitions and other war like materials while Pakistan had lagged behind. The choking of supplies of war material by the US and her Western Allies had made the Indian and Pakistan High Command take note of their logistical capabilities for the continuation of war. Logistics were no longer mere subservient to the operational dictates but were increasingly influencing the planning and conduct of war by late September of 1965.

Until the early sixties, Indian military's administrative infrastructure had been designed, in essence, to meet the requirements of a war against Pakistan in the West. With the emergence of China as a hostile neighbour, India split the existing administrative resources to meet the dual threat from China and Pakistan. As a result of the Sino-Indian border war, India established depots and administrative installations in Eastern India to secure self-sufficiency for troops deployed against the Chinese in the Himalayas. A large number of mountain divisions were raised. These were distinct from the infantry divisions and so were their operational roles, organisation, equipment and transport scales. The mountain divisions had no tanks and their artillery regiments had mountain guns with limited range and light shells. Due to reduced transport, the mountain divisions had serious limitations in plains against Pakistan. The expansion of the Army from nearly 3 to 8 lakhs, the introduction of a variety of weapons and equipment and the simultaneous decision to induct new equipment while phasing out old weapons, equipments and vehicles made equipping units and stocking depots complicated. The change over or introduction of new weapons and equipment had, of course, to be spread over a long period during which spares for the old and new equipments had to be available. The IAF also faced similar problems. Some of the new equipment had to be procured by developing indigenous sources while the rest came from abroad. Production in the factories, controlled by the Directorate General of Factories (DGOF), was geared up. A Heavy Vehicle Factory was set up at Avadi while Public Sector Undertakings producing defence material were expanded.

The US and her Western Allies had undertaken to give military aid to India after the Sino-Indian war but this was limited and strictly restricted to the operational requirements of mountain divisions facing the Chinese in the Himalayas. Tanks, anti-tank guns, field guns, and fighter aircraft were not supplied under pressure from Pakistan. Following the Indo-Pak hostilities, US and UK stopped military supplies and banned all sales of lethal weapons even by private agencies.

The Indian Army had been making do with World War weapons and equipment under the niggardly defence budget until 1962. The vehicle fleet suffered not only severe shortages and lack of spares, but many vehicles were old and unreliable. The situation was somewhat eased by the new discard policy which considered that the Army fleet needed only fully reliable and battle worthy vehicles. The rest were to be passed to the commercial agencies in a phased programme. To meet the requirements of the armed forces, DGOF organisation undertook vehicle production. The shortages were formidable even after nearly the whole production from Premier Automobiles and Mahindra and Mahindra were bought.

By 1965, the administrative set-up of Western Command was divided into two distinct geographical theatres. Punjab provided the support base for 11 Corps, while 15 Corps had its depots and administrative installations suitably located in the J&K State with the railhead at Pathankot. With the induction of 1 Corps into the Samba area, the existing administrative layout had to meet its logistical requirements until a Corps Maintenance Area (CMA) could be organised. It was decided to support 1 Corps from Pathankot with certain augmentations to develop it as an Army Maintenance Area (AMA).

New depots were hurriedly established in Pathankot to cater for the additional loads. 26 Infantry Division, operationally under I Corps, continued to be dependent on the depots in 15 Corps as hitherto. The Madhopur-Samba-Jammu road was earmarked for the exclusive use of 1 Corps while 15 Corps used the new Pathankot-Dhar-Udhampur road. Pathankot was an overcrowded place, being the railhead for 1 and 15 Corps, numerous depots, administrative installations and the air base. Previously the Pathankot administrative base was under 21 Communication Zone Sub Area under 15 Corps. It was shifted from 15 Corps to HQ Punjab and Himachal Pradesh Area for the coordination of 1 and 15 Corps' requirements. The depots in Pathankot AMA functioned as transit depots for 15 Corps, AMA for 1 Corps and also catered to the needs of about 18,000 garrison troops.

The army had no forward holdings of reserve tanks to replace tank casualties. 45 Cavalry, under raising at Babina, was moved to Delhi and at the last moment converted into an Armoured Delivery Regiment but without a kitting squadron. The result was that tanks that were despatched with deficient fire control instruments and other accessories could not quickly be made functional.

The handling of vehicle battle casualties posed a problem. 11 and 15 Corps had a Vehicle Company each while 1 Corps had none. Each Vehicle Company was able to establish only one Returned Vehicle Park which covered only one axis. After the battle of Asal Uttar, the area was littered with over a hundred abandoned or knocked out Pakistani tanks. These and other vehicles were collected in a central location near the battle area which became known as "Patton Nagar". 11 Corps Returned Vehicle Park was unable to move these to the rear areas.

1 Corps had no third line transport. Overall deficiency in I and 11 Corps was 900 vehicles. The operational requirement was to move forward three divisions and one armoured brigade in 11 Corps,

and one armoured, one infantry and one mountain division in 1 Corps simultaneously. Due to shortage of transport, the infantry division of 1 Corps could be moved only after the return of transport by 1 Corps after its first shift. With the help of the civil authorities, a fleet of over four thousand civilian vehicles was assembled in time for troops in 11 Corps to move to their battle locations from their peacetime locations. Similarly civilian vehicles were located at Pathankot and other places to move troops of 1 Corps. 6 Mountain Division alone needed 600 vehicles for its move forward from Ambala. Existing procedures for hiring civilian vehicles and making payments were modified to make the system quick and smooth to operate. Drivers of civilian vehicles were entitled to eat free food with their unit. Similarly they received medical facilities just like the jawans. Some civilian vehicles had to be used in front line units, their drivers working diligently in the forward areas. It was necessary to arrange ready payments for the requisitioned vehicles.

Along with the move forward of the troops, Army Maintenance Areas for 11 Corps were established on an ad hoc basis by 5 September, at Beas, Moga and Malout using civilian transport. A Control HQ for each of these was organised by 'milking' personnel from Signals, Army Service Corps, Medical, Ordnance, Electrical and Mechanical Engineers (EME), Provost units and 14 Gorkha Training Centre at Sabathu. From 6 September onwards ammunition, other stores and supplies went by rail at night beyond Ambala so that unloading at Pathankot and Jullunder could be completed before daylight. The Punjabi people rose to the occasion displaying inspiring patriotism. They provided voluntary labour, helped enthusiastically with refreshments and even carried ammunition to battle trenches.

To cater to battle casualties, the existing patients in Military Hospitals in Punjab and J&K were evacuated to hospitals in Delhi and beyond. Beds of the forward hospitals were increased to take the additional casualty load. The Punjab Government also offered beds in the civil hospitals.

From 6 September, battle casualties started coming quickly stretching existing resources in the forward hospitals to the limit. Ward coaches provided for the forward hospitals were found to be inadequate, so eventually ambulance trains were stabled at Amritsar, Ferozepur and Pathankot for the continuous evacuation of casualties to the rear hospitals. The existing staff at the military hospitals, in spite of working for nearly 18 hours daily, could not cope with the influx. Civilian doctors, surgeons and anaesthetists volunteered to help, providing much needed relief. Between 6 September and 23 September, the military hospitals in 1 and 11 Corps handled 6,100 battle casualties, and 6,500 non-battle casualties.

Dry rations posed no problem as Army HQ automatically sent special train loads for additional requirements to the forward supply depots without demands. Fresh supplies, on the other hand, were not available to new troops as the contractors could not supply, at short notice, more than 25% of the contract figures. The local Punjabi population organised cooked food for the troops in their areas. The milk shortage was met by milk powder from the Government Factory at Verka. Tinned substitutes made up for lack of fresh rations. The Army Service Corps handled a total of 46,000 tons of supplies and 44,000 tons of petroleum, oil and lubricants. In 1 and 11 Corps areas alone, Railhead Petroleum Depot, Pathankot received 11,000 tons and despatched 10,000 tons of FOL in 3,500 vehicles. General Transport Companies functioned without the relief driver increments. These were not sanctioned during the preparatory stage of the war so the relief drivers did not reach their units until hostilities had nearly ended.

A serious weak spot in the administrative plans was the mobilisation. No personnel, stores or vehicles had been earmarked for the Territorial Army (air defence or infantry units) including ordnance and ASC units. This affected the operational fitness of these units, particularly in the early stages of war. Even routine turnover of units had not been stopped so several units arrived in the Western Sector without essential equipment.

Ordnance establishments bear a heavy burden in the administrative support of the fighting machine. CODs had to work day and night, replenishing the forward ordnance depots (FODs) and replacing equipment of the formations, especially those entering the operational zone.

The availability of ammunition for actual fighting is a decisive factor in battle. The replenishment system of ammunition is well-regulated as the forward movement of ammunition is strictly related to the expenditure at the front, with each rearward echelon replenishing the next forward echelon. In actual practice, some extra movement of stocks was ordered as an insurance measure and some due to gross over-estimation of expenditure. This resulted in the forward move of far more ammunition than actually required. As the movement of ammunition from the rear depots involved very heavy tonnages, a number of special trains were run from distant places like Pulgaon (Madhya Pradesh) towards the depots in the Western theatre of war. As trains could run only at night, beyond Ambala, the railway network in the Punjab almost reached a breaking point.

1 FOD and 15 FAD (Forward Ammunition Depot) were well established to meet the requirements of the Jammu Sector to support the operations of the troops in the Jammu, Akhnoor and Poonch areas. These depots were well stocked to meet the needs of dependent troops if the Pathankot-Jammu road was temporarily cut off. 15 FAD issued 10,000 tons of ammunition and received an equal amount during 'Op Ablaze' and 'Op Riddle'. During the operation, 15 FAD established a sub-depot on the Pathankot-Dhar-Udhampur road. While 1 Corps depended for its maintenance on the AMA at Pathankot, 26 Infantry Division remained dependent for logistic support on 15 Corps depots as before.

2 FAD, with an ammunition sub-depot, provided administrative support to the troops in the Kashmir Valley. The ammunition sub-depot was attacked by infiltrators on 20 August and was defended by the few available troops from the perimeter trenches. By the time

it was attacked in strength on 23 August, a company of 6 Rajput had taken over the protection of the sub-depot, which handled 10,000 tons of ammunition during August and September.

3 FAD, established in East Punjab since 1948, was well located to meet the requirements of 11 Corps during operations. 17 FAD looked after its ammunition requirement, opened two sub-depots at Moga and Kasubegu and handled 17,000 tons of ammunition for 11 Corps during the war. On several occasions 17 FAD provided ammunition to 1 Corps too. The first 20 days War Wastage Reserve ammunition for 1 Armoured Division was despatched from 17 FAD on 4 September. 17 FAD handled a total of 56,000 tons of ammunition during the September war.

The ammunition requirement during the battle of Asal Uttar was heavy. 4 Division OMC had moved forward on 6 September while its ammunition platoon was in position on 4 September to issue the second line of ammunition to the division. The ammunition platoon worked day and night during the critical stage of the battle to ensure there was never any shortage of tank or artillery ammunition.

1 Corps had no suitably located FAD to meet their ammunition requirement. 15 FAD in Jammu Sector or 17 FAD in 11 Corps Sector were too far away to provide satisfactory ammunition backing. It was therefore decided to raise 18 FAD at a place suitable for 1 Corps. The reconnaissance for siting the FAD was carried out on 4 September at the height of operations in Chhamb Sector. The first instalment of the depot personnel and the military special ammunition trains for 18 FAD arrived on 6 September. In the absence of employed labour, the locals including students from the local school helped to unload these ammunition trains. Later on, immediate employment of 400 labourers was sanctioned. 150 combatant personnel of all ranks were moved in hired civilian buses from Jullundur to 18 FAD which started functioning by 12 September.

In war, artillery ammunition followed by fuel consumes

maximum tonnages. During a battle, guns move a number of times a day due to danger from counter-bombardment (CB), or other operational reasons. Large quantities of ammunition are frequently dumped at gun positions and on moving, the guns leave the ammunition behind to be picked up later. This compounds the problem of transport and troops for unloading/ loading of ammunition. Transport and gunner manpower is needed to service the current gun positions and stocking the next gun positions. The guns keep on moving from gun pit to gun pit. Some guns have to fire excessive amounts of ammunition while the others fire very little on certain days. In a high intensity war, large amounts of unexpended ammunition is thus left scattered over the battlefield while the units keep on drawing ammunition from the Ordnance depots. The ammunition situation thus becomes confused which is further aggravated by heavy accumulations in the forward installations. Such a situation thus gives an unrealistic impression of expenditure and state of holdings at higher HQs.

OBSERVATIONS, COMMENTS AND LESSONS

Strategy

A major national war aim of Pakistan was the annexation of Jammu and Kashmir, by force. As has been brought out earlier, the Kashmir Issue remained dormant for a considerable period after 1949, because of Pakistan's intransigence, in not implementing the Security Council's Resolution of August 13, 1948, which called for withdrawal of her forces from Pakistan Occupied Kashmir. During the period, India held three General Elections in Kashmir (including one for Constitutional Assembly), where people turned up in large numbers and exercised their franchise without fear or favour. In these, they gave a constitution for themselves and elected Governments of their choice. Thus the Security Council Resolution with regard to the Plebiscite in Kashmir became irrelevant After President Ayub came to power, he decided to reactivate the Kashmir Issue. General Mohammad Musa, the then Pakistani Commander-in-Chief, stated that Mr. Zulfiqar Ali Bhutto, the Foreign Minister and other Advisors of President Ayub, pressurised him (the President) to take advantage of the disturbed situation in the Valley and direct the Army to send raiders into Indian-held Kashmir for conducting guerrilla activities there for establishing bases and for helping the locals in organising a movement with a view to eventually staging an uprising against the occupying power. He says, "According to them, steps taken by the Director Intelligence Bureau (DIB) till then were not only ineffective but had also alerted the army of occupation which as a consequence had tightened its suppressive and security measures". He further says, "but we were directed to prepare two plans for action in Kashmir—an all out one and another in a lower key". He goes on, "later, during the third week of August, as far as I remember, we received another brief Presidential Directive stating that steps be taken to de-freeze the Kashmir issue in which the Army should take an active part".

This indicates the strategic thinking of the Pakistani High Command. Musa himself was not in favour of launching the infiltration operation at the time as "in the first place, adequate preparations had not been made in the Valley to start guerrilla activity. We had not even apprised the local pro-Pakistan leaders of our intention and plan of action nor ascertained from them whether they would be willing to and could help us in any way". Despite advice to the contrary from Musa, it would appear that the decision was taken to launch the guerrilla war. When the guerrillas could not get any significant help from the local population of Kashmir and India was able to frustrate the evil designs of the Pakistanis. Pakistan launched a major attack across the International border on Chhamb. It was clear that after this, India could not confine its counter measures to Jammu and Kashmir only as it would have meant fighting in an area disadvantageous to her and also, in the process, exposing her heartland to undue risks. In any case, India had made it clear several times that an attack on Kashmir would be treated as an attack on India and that she would take counter action accordingly. Thus, after the Chhamb attack, India quite rightly retaliated in

Punjab. If was also clear that, in view of the arrogance of Pakistan brought about by the receipt of massive military aid from the United States of America, unless her wings were clipped, she would continue to pose a serious threat to Kashmir. It was thus decided to carry the war into Pakistan territory and inflict maximum possible attrition, on her armed might. Capture of any territory in the process, was only of secondary importance. In this connection it would be pertinent to mention General Chaudhuri's views on the military aim and strategy during this war. In his autobiography, he states:

> "In 1964, when we were revising military plans to defend ourselves in case of an attack from our neighbour, the troops available on the Western Front in effective numbers were roughly equivalent to those of Pakistan.
>
> ...In the limited advance which must form the fulcrum of any defensive plan, we were faced with three alternatives. The first one was the occupation of some unguarded territory. This second was the occupation of and probably substantial destruction to a big city. For this, there were insufficient troops.
>
> In dealing with this alternative, there was also the political view that any substantial destruction of a major population and historical centre would leave a raw wound between two neighbours, delaying unduly the eventual aim of living in amity. The third alternative was the destruction of equipment cheaply obtained, but if destroyed, expensive in every way to replace. The third alternative seemed the correct choice. I would submit that we were successful in the pattern we adopted and the ensuing heavy economic burden and political disturbances in Pakistan certainly contributed to the downfall of the Ayub Government
>
> ...To capture Lahore was not the aim of 1965 operations. Our experience has shown that taking any such large town would require a very large number of troops and the process would involve destruction of the town on a large scale which would not be a good thing for the future. My aim was only to destroy the Pakistani fighting potential, that is, the equipment and trained forces and in this I feel I succeeded. We played havoc with Pakistani tanks and I think this action alone was probably responsible for removing Field Marshal Ayub Khan from the position of Head of State.

As has been brought out, considerable attrition was inflicted on

Pakistan, although in the process. India also suffered fairly significant casualties. This had compelled Pakistan, apart from other factors, to agree to a ceasefire and withdrawal of forces. The main point that comes out, therefore, is that India evolved the correct strategy for herself and adhered to it. As for Pakistan, she had miscalculated India's likely response and under-estimated her military capabilities. Although Musa says that an Indian counter offensive was expected in the Punjab, the fact remains that Pakistan was unable to meet it adequately and at the same time achieve its war aim with regard to Jammu and Kashmir.

Maintenance of the Aim

In this war, Pakistan's initial aim was to secure Jammu and Kashmir by the force of arms. She attempted large scale infiltration, with the hope of fomenting a revolt inside Jammu and Kashmir but had not carried out the necessary preparations. Subsequently, when India took counter action across the International Border, Pakistan attempted to secure Indian territory up to the Beas river and later exploit further. She was not able to achieve either of her aims, as both the operations petered out for various reasons, as brought out.

On the Indian side, the aim was to remain on offensive defence in Jammu and Kashmir, while launching a limited offensive into Punjab across the International Border, In the Lahore Sector, the aim was to secure the Ichhogil Canal and pose a threat to Lahore, while in the Sialkot Sector, the aim was to drive a wedge between the Lahore and Sialkot Sectors and neutralize Sialkot. While the initial operations went off well, owing to incorrect reaction by some of the commanders to the Pakistani counter action, the objective (Ichhogil canal) was lost after its capture. Subsequently, however, it was partially recovered, at considerable cost. In the Sialkot Sector, while the performance was better, the final objectives could not be captured. Of course, the offensive could not develop its full potential due to inadequate time available before the cease fire.

The need for pursuing the aim relentlessly requires little stress.

There is no doubt that this factor influenced the ultimate stalemate, to a considerable extent.

Guerrilla Operations

Experience not only in India but throughout the world has shown that, for a guerrilla war to succeed, the support of the local population is an essential pre-requisite. In the case of Jammu and Kashmir, Pakistan could not receive such support, Because of the provocative statements of some Kashmiri leaders, because of some local disturbances caused by the temporary loss of a relic (hair of Prophet Mohammad) from the Hazaratbal Mosque, and because of the fissiparous tendencies that surfaced in India after Shastri took over as Prime Minister, Pakistan miscalculated that the time was ripe for starting a guerrilla movement in Kashmir. By infiltrating large numbers of irregular forces, and by backing with regular forces at a later stage, Pakistan hoped to annex Kashmir by force, in conjunction with an 'uprising' in Kashmir. As General Musa points out, neither any effort was made to check whether the local people would support such a movement, nor were any preparations made within Kashmir, for the success of such a concept. Apart from a few odd people, who had pro-Pakistani leanings, the bulk of the people had, in fact, supported the Indian Army in its counter infiltration operations. Otherwise, it would have been extremely difficult for the Indian Army to defend Kashmir, without the willing support of the local population. Most of the infiltrators were eliminated or apprehended, mainly due to the information given by the locals. Further, considerable logistic support was provided by the local people, in the way of porters, ponies, other transport and so on. The Civil Administration, which comprised mostly the local people, was fully behind the Armed Forces. All these would not have been possible, had the allegations in some quarters, that India was holding Kashmir by force, were true. On the other hand, because of the considerable autonomy that the State enjoyed within the Indian Union and because of the significant progress achieved by the State all-round since accession, the people felt as nationalistic as anyone else in the rest of India and aligned themselves fully behind the war effort.

Offensive Operations

The results achieved by the Pakistan offensive in the Chhamb Sector were impressive, but the advantage was not fully exploited by Pakistan, to capture Akhnoor. In the subsequent counter offensive launched by India in Punjab from the East, though some success was achieved in that most of the troops initially got to their objective, namely, the Ichhogil Canal, it soon petered out; and many of the forces were more or less thrown back to the start line. Subsequently, with great effort, some of the forces managed to re-take some of their objectives, particularly in the 15 Divisional Sector. In the case of 4 Division, there was a near catastrophe. It would appear that their offensive was neither well planned nor executed with the determination and aggressiveness that it warranted. Troops were brought from peace time cantonments and launched into operations, without adequate reconnaissance, preparations, fire support, logistic support and effective coordination. The main consideration appeared to be achievement of surprise. In peace time, operational plans should have been drawn up and rehearsed in own territory; as is normally done. In this case, perhaps, the time available was limited, but even so, the broad strategic response to a Pakistani attack in Kashmir, was well known. Based on this, the necessary preparations could have been carried out better.

In the case of 1 Corps operations from the North into Punjab, these were better executed, although the time available here also was limited and not adequate preparations could have been made. The very concentration of this whole Corps for its offensive in the battle area, in reasonable time, was a feat of no mean magnitude. In the actual implementation of the plan, it has to be realised that ultimately the bulk of the Pakistan armour was poised against the Corps. Further, monsoon rains had made the ground soggy and difficult for movement. However, from time to time, confusion occurred among the forces due to inadequate coordination. It had later transpired that the Pakistani 6 Armoured Division had not concentrated in the Sialkot Sector till 9 September and that the Indian offensive was really opposed by the integral armour of the defensive formations. On this, Colonel S.C. Mehdi wrote, "If Pakistan ever had divine protection, it was on that night and forty-eight hours of 8/9 September because, had the Indian armour broken through, the consequences would have been as disastrous for Pakistan as the German Panzers' breakthrough in France in 1940". If this was correct, it would appear that if the Indian offensive pressed on more vigorously in the early stages, it might have achieved much better results.

The Pakistan counter-offensive in Khemkaran Sector was also not well planned nor efficiently executed. After securing a lodgement, a valuable twenty-four hours were lost before resuming the offensive. The momentum was thus halted and the Indian 4 Mountain Division utilised the vital respite to reorganize itself. Subsequently, after the offensive was resumed, it was not pressed home. As General Musa pointed out, there was no excuse for troops to have fallen back, after securing or nearly securing their objectives. The Pakistani Armoured Division confined itself to a narrow corridor, the defence of which was well organised by 4 Division and 2 Independent Armoured Brigade. There has been considerable criticism of the failure of the Pakistani counter-offensive in Khemkaran, among Pakistani circles. Air Marshal Asghar Khan (earlier Chief of the Pakistani Air Force) considers that, "the detachment of 7 Infantry Division from 1 Armoured Division with which it had been preparing for a crucial offensive South of Lahore was an unmitigated blunder." He also felt that there were serious lacunas in inter-Service cooperation. He was of the opinion that Ayub Khan had no understanding of the concept of air operations and little understanding of the maritime interests. Brigadier Riazul Karim considers that there was inadequate reconnaissance, poor stage management and ineffective control on the operations. He also focuses attention on the lack of coordination between 1 Armoured Division and 11 Infantry Division. Lieutenant Colonel Irshad Rashid brings out the absence of a Corps

Headquarters for controlling this vital offensive, the control having been exercised by GHQ direct. Lieutenant General Attiqur Rahman in his book *Our Defence Cause* brings out that. "Our counter-offensive in the Khemkaran area failed after such a promising start chiefly because it lacked a suitable Headquarters."

General Musa, in support of his claim of achievements of the aborted Khemkaran offensive, quotes General Kaul's book that the Indian Army Chief, General Chaudhuri, had ordered the Army Commander to withdraw behind the Beas river. However, there is really no evidence to this effect. General Chaudhari, who was considered an armour expert of repute, knew the potential of the defence, particularly of 2 Independent Armoured Brigade against the 1 Armoured Division of Pakistan. Further, certain contingency planning to hold any breakthrough behind 4 Mountain Division, was carried out by 11 Corps and necessary troops earmarked for the purpose. Even if the odd enemy tank got through, these would have been effectively dealt with. Thus, it is inconceivable that a knowledgeable person like General Chaudhari would have ever issued any such orders. The very fact that Pakistan had to shift the bulk of this armoured division to the Sialkot Sector shows the havoc that the Indian offensive there would have played behind the Pakistani lines. Thus, even if Pakistan achieved some success at Khemkaran, it would have been more than compensated for by the Indian offensive in the Sialkot Sector. Lahore might have been completely isolated and might have been seriously threatened. This should be seen in the light of the fact that, in the early stages of the Indian counter-offensive, Lahore was evacuated to some extent and Indian permission had to be sought by foreign planes to land at Lahore airport.

To revert to the Indian side, subsequently Divisional-sized counter-offensives by 4 Division and 10 Division also met with no success, due to inadequate' preparations. These were launched within a matter of twenty-four hours or so.

All these bring out the need for pre-planning to the extent possible during peace time, subsequent refining of plans when the actual war starts, adequate reconnaissance and preparations, thorough coordination and vigorous execution of plans. Some of the other points needing attention, that came out were as under:

(a) Re-organisation on a captured objective must be carried out speedily and efficiently.

(b) Armour must move to the captured objective at the earliest, in order to prevent enemy armour overrunning the captured objective.

(c) Subsequent phases of an attack must be launched without loss of time.

(d) Commanders must be well forward, in order to acquaint themselves with the developing situation and to take speedy decisions.

(e) Frontal attack should be avoided. The potential of outflanking movement must be fully exploited.

(f) Bold use should be made of armour, to achieve worthwhile results. Cooperation between infantry and tanks should be intimate.

(g) Failures should not be reinforced, to the extent possible. On the other hand, success should be exploited, to achieve the ultimate aim of the commander.

(h) Fire plan must be thoroughly coordinated and adequate support ensured for an attack.

(i) An attack must always be launched from a secure base.

Defensive Operations

In Jammu and Kashmir, India chose to remain basically on the defensive. Despite large scale infiltration by Pakistan, and despite being cut off or the threat of being cut off, the Indian forces held to their ground, unlike what happened in the Kameng Sector in 1962. Further, it was also realised that, for defence to be successful, a certain amount of local offensive operations have to be launched; in other words, it had to be offensive defence. Thus, the capture of Hajipir which had not only resulted in capturing a major base of Pakistani operations, but had also relieved pressure in other sectors, was a significant achievement for the Indian Army. The capture of the Bugina Bulge in the Tithwal sector, was a creditable achievement too. In the Turtok sector in the North also, a local offensive prevented the Pakistanis from posing any serious threat to Ladakh or against the communications to Ladakh.

Some of the important lessons that came out of defensive operations were as under:

(a) In the plains, the positions selected should be such, that outflanking movements should not be possible.

(b) When a defensive position is to be occupied at short notice in the face of the enemy, adequate elements must be deployed forward to delay the enemy and to gain the requisite time for preparations of the defences.

(c) The vital need for speedily digging down, in order to minimise casualties, cannot be overemphasised.

(d) Effective coordination must be carried out to the extent possible, even if time is short. In particular, maximum fire support should be available at the point of attack by the enemy.

(e) The main thrust of the enemy must be carefully discerned, before deciding to commit the reserve.

(f) Defence must be carried out aggressively and maximum attrition imposed on the enemy.

(g) The importance of aggressive patrolling and tank hunting.

(h) The need for timely and accurate intelligence about enemy concentrations, particularly his armour.

(i) Troops must be trained to withstand heavy artillery and tank fire. For this purpose, battle inoculation during peace time is important

Intelligence

It has been brought out that large numbers of irregular forces were infiltrated into Jammu and Kashmir during the period August 5 to 10, 1965, in columns of 600 or more. It had later transpired that the recruitment, training and organisation for infiltration operations started as early as May 1965. Yet, no clear assessment of Pakistan's intention to launch a large-scale infiltration campaign in Jammu and Kashmir in this manner was ever made by our Intelligence Agencies. Similarly, it was reiterated that Pakistani 1 Armoured Division had moved to Kharian after 'Op Ablaze' whereas it was discovered later that the Division had stayed back in area Raiwind. The fact that Pakistani 6 Armoured Division was equipped with Patton tanks was also not known, nor that they had raised four tank destroyer units. The concentration of Pakistani 7 Infantry Division for attack on Chhamb, was also not known. The raising of 11 Division was not brought to notice either.

As far as Pakistan was concerned, despite the Indian Prime Minister declaring openly to the effect that India would retaliate wherever it suits her, the Pakistan Army was not properly prepared for an Indian attack across the International Border in the Lahore Sector. Defences on the Ichhogil Canal were not manned, when Indian forces reached the line on the night of 5/6 September and the Lahore Divisional Commander as well as his Division were still reportedly in the cantonment area during that night. It was only on the morning of 6 September that the formation reacted. In this connection, Brigadier Riazul Karim (retired) wrote, "In the Lahore sector, it was Allah who saved us by making the Indians falter on their own and stop at the Batapur canal thinking there was some trap laid on by the Pakistan forces. On receiving flash information from our screen, troops located on the canal banks, our main forces, went forward on 6th morning after they had done their morning PT in the unit lines". Another writer Colonel Irshad Rashad (retired) stated, "It would not be incorrect to say in all honesty that on the night of 5/6 September, when the Indians attacked, the bulk of the forward divisions of the Pakistan Army were not in their battle locations", Further, from the panic reactions in the Sialkot Sector, it is apparent that Pakistan did not have adequate information of the Indian 1 Corps thrusts from the Jammu sector on 8 September.

From the above examples, it would be apparent that a lot was left to be desired on both sides, as far as intelligence was concerned

Surprise

Despite the Indian Prime Minister's open declaration that India would retaliate wherever it chooses to, the Pakistani high command was surprised when an actual attack was launched by India across the International Border on the night of 5/6 September. This was mainly due a mental fixation that India may not actually do so, due to likely international repercussions, Of course, lack of intelligence also contributed to this situation. On the other hand, Indian forces achieved initial surprise, but did not exploit the situation, due to clumsy handling by some local commanders in the Lahore Sector. Equally, while initial surprise was achieved in the Sialkot Sector, it was not fully exploited due to inadequate boldness and aggressiveness in the handling of armour. Earlier, Indian Forces allowed themselves to be surprised by the Pakistani infiltration into Jammu and Kashmir, as well as by the attack on Chhamb. As the Kashmir question remains unresolved, the threat of infiltration, which is a low-cost option, would always be there; and appropriate and effective measures need to be taken, to prevent it from succeeding.

Unity of Command

One of the main reasons for the initial success of infiltration into Jammu and Kashmir was because the various agencies responsible for dealing with the threat, were functioning on their own. These included the Army, the Jammu and Kashmir Militia, the Armed Police Battalions, the Jammu and Kashmir Police and so on. Each of these forces had their own control Headquarters and were receiving conflicting directions, or in some cases inadequate guidance. To deal with a threat of the magnitude that took place, it was obvious that all the forces should have been put under the operational control of the local Army formation commanders, so that their actions could be fully coordinated and an integrated plan could be evolved and implemented.

Entity of Formations

In this war, almost all the Divisions of 11 Corps functioned with only two brigades under command, the third brigade having been assigned other tasks. Thus, when attacks were held up, they found themselves at a disadvantage, due to the lack of the requisite reserves. There were of course, the problems of shortage of troops to man the long border, as well as lack of adequate reserves at the Corps level. There were other deficiencies too, such as non-availability of an integral armoured regiment in the infantry division, non-availability of a medium artillery regiment and so on. 4 Mountain Division had its own organisational weaknesses, being a Mountain Division with a task in the plains. A number of these deficiencies have been made up, or are being made up. It must be ensured that a formation's or a unit's entity is always maintained. Any detachment should be an exception rather than the rule. Equally, if a Mountain Division has an alternative role in the plains, the requisite equipment for plains warfare must be catered for and the necessary training imparted for the purpose.

Effect of Weather

One of the considerations with regard to the timing of a war has always been the question of suitability of the weather. This war was fought towards the later part of the monsoon. Owing to the ground conditions, the offensive operations were adversely affected to some extent. The ground imposes serious constraints on the employment of armour. However, it has to be remembered that in between the spells of rain, if there is a long enough gap, some movement does become possible. There is also the problem of the numerous innocent-looking streams, and minor rivers which become heavily flooded soon after a rain, but become passable after a suitable lapse of time. It would thus be incorrect, to rule out military operations altogether, during the monsoon period. Equally, it has to be accepted that certain constraints would be imposed by weather on the smooth conduct of operations.

Air Support

During this war, it was felt that air support was inadequate. Substantial part of it was apparently directed towards strategic tasks and air defence. Thus, for close support of the Army, sufficient air support was not forthcoming. The available air effort was kept centralised at Advance Headquarters Western Air Command and it took time for formations to receive air support. Further, the aircraft were moved to airfields well away from the theatre, for reasons of security. There were other weaknesses, such as unsatisfactory communications between JOCs and airfields, limited range of wireless sets, inexperienced officers with ACTs, inadequate training in aircraft recognition and so on. The problem of enemy aircraft being superior in some respects was also there. Many of these weaknesses were remedied subsequently after the war.

The Navy

In this war, ships of the Indian Navy maintained vigil and ensured the defence of sea lanes and shore facilities. There were, however, no clashes with the Pakistani Navy.

Logistics

A major achievement of the Indians was the concentration of 1 Corps in the Jammu Sector at very short notice, from its peace time locations in Central India. This was done very efficiently, with the help of the railways and civilian transport from States. As Indian cantonments are far away from the borders, this will always be a basic requirement in a war. The need for proper planning of moves during peace, and cooperation and coordination between various agencies at the imminence of a war, cannot be-overemphasised. The Railways, Airlines and State Governments have an important responsibility in this regard.

Enemy Tactical Concepts

Originally, the technical concepts followed both by India and Pakistan, were based on the British Indian Army concepts. However, after receipt of significant military assistance from the USA, including training facilities, there was a change in the Pakistani tactical concepts. These were more of the American type, which are somewhat different from the British type, for various reasons. In the 1965 War, these concepts came to light for the first time. It may be mentioned that in the 1962 War, the Chinese tactical concepts also came to light for the first time. All these bring out the need for studying the potential adversaries in a comprehensive manner during peace time. This will ensure that troops are not surprised when the war starts.

Equipment

In this war, Pakistan entered the field with superior military equipment. In fact, one of the main reasons for her starting the war was the perceived qualitative superiority of her personnel and equipment over the Indians. On the Indian side, the arms and equipment were still of Second World War Vintage due to which the troops were at a disadvantage. However, the Pakistani personnel found it difficult to handle the sophisticated armour (Patton tanks), as opposed to the Indians who, though equipped with older Centurions and Shermans, managed to get the first shot in. This brings out the need for proper training of personnel. The requirement of up-to-date equipment for a modem army is of course unexceptionable. Further, it would be wrong to assume that Pakistan has not learnt its lesson. In case of a future confrontation, it should be accepted that their personnel would be well trained in handling the equipment at their disposal. There should be no complacency in this regard.

Leadership

It would be interesting to carry out a broad analysis of the leadership on both sides, in this war.

On the Pakistani side, Field Marshal Ayub Khan, the President, had a military background, and when he seized power, was generally accepted by the nation as one who could bring stability and protect and promote the interests of his country. Although he is supposed to have rejected an earlier plan for massive infiltration into Kashmir, he is reported to have agreed to revive the plan in 1965 for various reasons which were considered to be favourable for Pakistan. The reverses suffered by India during the Chinese invasion of 1962, the willingness shown by India during talks with Pakistan to make adjustments on the cease fire line in Kashmir, the disturbed situation in India after the death of Nehru and the coming into power of Shastri as the Prime Minister, the aid provided by the US to India after the Chinese Aggression whereby India could become stronger, the disturbed situation in Kashmir as a result of the theft of the holy relic and alleged closer integration of Kashmir with India, the performance of Pakistani forces in Kutch with modern US equipment and the limited Indian reaction, the anticipated help from the Chinese and other Allies, and the assessment that India would not retaliate across the International Border were some of the reasons which prompted Ayub to defreeze the situation and attempt 'liberation' of Kashmir.

There are also other reasons given by certain Pakistani leaders and writers, the chief of which was that Bhutto planned to project himself into power, by involving Ayub in a war which he could not win! Whatever be the reasons, Ayub had obviously miscalculated and underestimated Indian capabilities and reactions. General Musa, the Commander-in-Chief, was apparently against the Kashmir adventure, but still went along with it.

There are allegations that he had not given proper directions to meet the inevitable counter-offensive by the Indians. His earlier Chief of Staff, Lieutenant General Habibulla Khan Khattak (retired) wrote,

"The forward battle formation kept on requesting permission to move into forward battle positions: but there were firm negative orders from the Army Chief." The counter-offensive that he planned and launched in the Lahore sector failed. His reaction to the Indian advance from Jammu area into the Sialkot Sector, was panicky. At the lower levels, Lieutenant General Akhtar Hussain Malik, was removed from command after the failure of the infiltration operation. Major General Yahya Khan, the 7 Divisional Commander, initially displayed competence and aggressive spirit in capturing Chhamb-Jaurian but could not secure the ultimate objective—Akhnoor. He is reported to have said that he was dissuaded from doing so. In the Sialkot sector, Lieutenant General Bakhtiar Rana performed reasonably well, in that he prevented the Indians getting to their final objectives. In the Lahore Sector, the performance of the commanders including Major General Abdul Hamid, the ad hoc force commander, was inadequate. The Armoured Divisional Commander, Major General Nazir Ahmed Khan, had not displayed adequate professionalism and aggressiveness, due to which his operation failed. Maybe, he was let down by his subordinate commanders.

On the Indian side, the leadership was better. General Chaudhuri, the Chief of the Army Staff was experienced, competent and realistic. His reaction to a Pakistani adventure in Jammu and Kashmir, was absolutely correct, namely, a counter-offensive across the International Border. He ensured that the offensives were launched as planned, although all the objectives were not secured. The main achievement was that the better pan of the fighting was done in Pakistan territory and considerable losses were inflicted on the Pakistanis, particularly of war-like equipment. Lieutenant General. Harbakhsh Singh, the Army Commander Western Command, who was responsible for the main fighting, was cool, competent and aggressive, and inspired tremendous confidence among the subordinates and the troops. Lieutenant General Dunn, the Corps Commander in the Jammu sector, was a professional, who earlier on blunted the enemy in Kutch and provided proper directions and guidance to his Corps in the offensive. In the 11 Corps sector, General Dhillon was aggressive, but there was some crisis of confidence, due to the removal of a number of formation and unit commanders. In the 15 Corps sector, Lieutenant General K.S. Katoch stood like a rock and more than compensated for any losses he suffered. Among the Divisional Commanders, particular mention needs to be made of Major General. Gurbakhsh Singh, the General Officer Commanding 4 Mountain Division. But for his correct appreciation, timely occupation of the Asal Uttar position and aggressive conduct of the defensive battle in conjunction with 2 Independent Armoured Brigade, the Pakistani Armoured thrust could well have got through and created an extremely difficult and unenviable situation for the Indians. At the lower levels, the quality of leadership varied from very good to weak in some cases. Some of the lower commanders tried to control battles from their Headquarters, instead of going forward.

BATTLE OF HAJIPIR PASS

Background

The cease-fire of 1 January 1949 ended the First Kashmir War but did nothing to improve the relations between Pakistan and India. Kashmir remained the bone of contention. Nehru offered a no war pact to Pakistan. Pakistan said that such a pact could only be signed after an honourable solution of the Kashmir issue. Thus while India sought peace and development, Pakistan sought Kashmir and to build a military capability strong enough to defeat India.

In the early fifties, United States, in a bid to contain the Soviet Union and spread of communism, formed a number of regional military groups like the North Atlantic Treaty Organisation (NATO), Central Treaty Organisation (CENTO) and South East Asian Treaty Organisation (SEATO). The concept was that each member would pour in resources (mainly manpower resources) for collective defence of the area against the Soviet threat and spread of communism.

In return, United States pledged to assist the member states economically and militarily. This provided Pakistan an opportunity to strengthen its armed forces at minimal cost. Pakistan joined CENTO and SEATO in September 1955. India, under Nehru, the architect of the Non-Aligned Movement, chose to remain non-aligned. Pakistan benefited greatly from joining the mutual defence treaties sponsored by US. In the period between 1954 to 1965, Pakistan received military aid worth $ 1.5 billion. The equipment included Patton tanks, Sabre jets, FI04 Star Fighter aircraft, MI rifles, Universal machine guns, mortars, recoilless rifles, guns and every other conceivable type of defence equipment.

The Pakistan Army officers received training in United States and Britain and joint military exercises were carried out. Thus, by 1965, Pakistan had completely modernised its armed forces with new equipment received from the United States. It had also been able to upgrade the so-called Azad Kashmir forces or forces in Pakistan Occupied Kashmir. Pakistan had also concluded a treaty of cooperation in military and economic affairs with China.

The armed forces had taken over Pakistan Government after a military coup in October 1958. General Ayub Khan became the new president of Pakistan. By 1965, Pakistan was ready for another war with India.

On 9 April 1965, 51 Infantry Brigade of the Pakistan Army crossed the international border into the Rann of Kutch and captured Sardar Post near Kanjarkot. On 24 April Pakistan attacked again with tanks and artillery and captured four more posts and the entire Kanjarkot area. The Indian Army did not put up any significant fight and withdrew. Possibly it was surprised and not in a position to resist. It was reasoned that the monsoon flooding of the Rann of Kutch would, in any case, drive the Pakistani Army out. It was also not militarily and logistically prepared to drive out the Pakistani forces.

Soon after capturing the Kanjarkot area, Pakistan offered to negotiate. India refused saying that there could be no talks till Pakistan vacated the areas illegally occupied. However, Shastri met

Ayub Khan at the Commonwealth Conference in London. Under the influence of the British Prime Minister, a cease-fire agreement was signed on 30 June. Under the agreement Pakistan agreed to withdraw its forces and restore Indian control over the area. India agreed to allow Pakistan to use a road it had constructed in Indian Territory.

In April 1965, along with the invasion in Kutch, Ayub activated the cease-fire line (CFL) in Jammu & Kashmir and there were many cease-fire violations. Next, in May, Pakistan launched operations at Kargil to cut-off the Srinagar – Leh road. Pakistani infiltrators crossed the CFL and occupied three high hill features astride the Highway and established observation posts.

From these observation posts, they brought down accurate artillery fire on the road and disrupted the traffic. India reacted by complaining to the UN observers. Nothing happened. The Indian Army then launched operations to evict the intruders. This was successfully done on 17 May 1965. However, the positions were vacated in June 1965 when UN Observers were posted in the area.

While a cease-fire was being negotiated in Kutch, Pakistan was preparing for its next attempt to capture Kashmir. This was to be achieved through clandestine infiltration of a large number of guerrillas in early August 1965. The operation was code named OPERATION GIBRALTAR.

The designated forces were to infiltrate in small groups and concentrate on 7 August, mingle with the crowds to celebrate the festival of Pir Dastagir Sahib on 8 August. Next day, they were to mingle with crowds assembling to demonstrate against the arrest of Sheikh Abdullah and commence operations. It was a bold and brilliant plan. The Indian intelligence had failed to obtain any specific information about it. But fortunately for India and unfortunately for Pakistan, the plan misfired.

On 5 August, two infiltrators in green *salwar kameez* approached a young shepherd near Gulmarg and offered him money for some information. The individual immediately reported the matter to

Tangmarg Police Station. The same day a few infiltrators approached a local man in Mendhar area for some information. The local reported the matter to the nearby brigade headquarters. The alerted Indian Army captured two officers on 8 August near Narian. Their interrogation revealed the whole plan. Some incidents of firing and subversive activities were reported during 10 to 12 August.

Security forces throughout the length and breadth of the State were alerted. A counter operation was launched against the infiltrators. Without local support they had nowhere to go. They were stalked, engaged and liquidated piecemeal. They were completely demoralised. Some surrendered; some exfiltrated across the CFL; and large quantities of arms and ammunition were captured. OPERATION GIBRALTAR had collapsed by 12 August.

While the mopping up operations were going on, Shastri made an unambiguous statement. He said that if necessary India may attack raiders' bases and the tussle may last long. He also said, "India cannot go on pushing the Pakistanis off its territory. If infiltration continues, we will have to carry the fight to the other side." The Indian Army had also concluded that the only way to stop infiltration was to retaliate by crossing the CFL boldly and plugging the routes used by the raiders and the areas used by their supporters. This' plan was put into operation on 15 August in the Kargil Sector. The Indian troops crossed the CFL and recaptured the three Pakistani positions, which had been captured by them and vacated in May. Some heights in Tithwal and Uri Sectors were also captured. India also decided to capture the Hajipir Bulge, which was an important hub of Pakistani infiltration operations against India.

The task of capturing Hajipir Pass and the Bulge was given to 19 Infantry Division and the corps reserve of 68 Infantry Brigade was placed under the command of 19 Infantry Division for the operation which was code named OP BAKSHI. 25 Infantry Division was given the task of linking up with the force from Poonch under code name OP FAULAD.

Relative Strengths

About one brigade of the enemy including some battalions held the Hajipir Bulge. Of this about one battalion was holding the northern approaches to the pass. The assessed disposition of the enemy is shown on Map No 10. The troops had well prepared defences and were supported by artillery.

The following troops were placed under command of 68 Infantry Brigade for the capture of Hajipir Pass:

1 PARA
19 PUNJAB
4 RAJPUT
6 JAK RIF
4 SIKH LI
164 Field Regiment less one battery (12 field guns)
144 Mountain Battery (6 howitzers)
B Troop 39 Medium Regiment (3 medium guns)
18 Field Battery (6 field guns)
One section of 4.2 inch mortars

The Plan

It was appreciated that a frontal assault on the pass astride the Uri-Poonch track would be very costly in terms of casualties and unlikely to succeed. The eviction of the enemy by an indirect and difficult approach was considered to have better chances. The plan of action envisaged a pincer movement from the west and east converging on Hajipir. To keep the enemy guessing about Indian intentions and to tie down his reserves, the following diversionary attacks were planned:

(a) 7 BIHAR (161 Infantry Brigade) was to capture Tilpatra and Ziarat by first light D-day and Burji on Night D-day plus 1.

(b) 6 DOGRA (41 Mountain Brigade) was to capture Mehandi Gali and Lunda on the night of D-day plus 1.

The plan for capture of Hajipir on the Sank or western approach was as under:

(a) 1 PARA was to capture Sank and Lediwali Gali by 0500 hours on D-day plus 1.

(b) 4 RAJPUT was to pass through 1 PARA and capture Hajipir Pass by 1800 hours D-day plus 1.

The plan of attack on the Bedori or eastern approach was that 19 PUNJAB would capture Ring Contour, Pathra and Point 12330 (Bedori feature) by 0900 hours D-day plus 1. Thereafter, 19 PUNJAB was to exploit up to Point 11107 and establish contact with 1 PARA by 1800 hours on D-day plus 1.

6 JAK RIF and 4 SIKH LI were held in reserve. The D-day was initially fixed as 25 August 1965. Due to heavy rain it was postponed to 26 August.

The Battle

68 Infantry Brigade crossed the CFL in two columns on 26 August. 1 PARA crossed to the west and commenced its attack on Sank; a formidable feature with well prepared defences, barbed wire and mines, at 2130 hours. The Brigade Commander, Brigadier Z. C. Bakshi, accompanied the assaulting troops. It was raining heavily and it was a difficult climb. The attack was silent. The troops reached the top of the feature at 0415 hours next morning.

The enemy were completely surprised and fled leaving behind their heavy weapons including two machine guns and three light machine guns. The battalion continued exploitation without giving the enemy any chance to reorganise and put up a fight. They rushed Sar, the next feature and captured it by 0930 hours on 28 August. They pressed on, and all areas up to and including Ledi Wali Gali were captured by 1800 hours on 27 August. The Indian casualties in the attack were 21 wounded. The enemy casualties were 10 killed, 40 wounded and one taken prisoner.

Major Ranjit Singh Dayal, who was the hero of the battle, asked

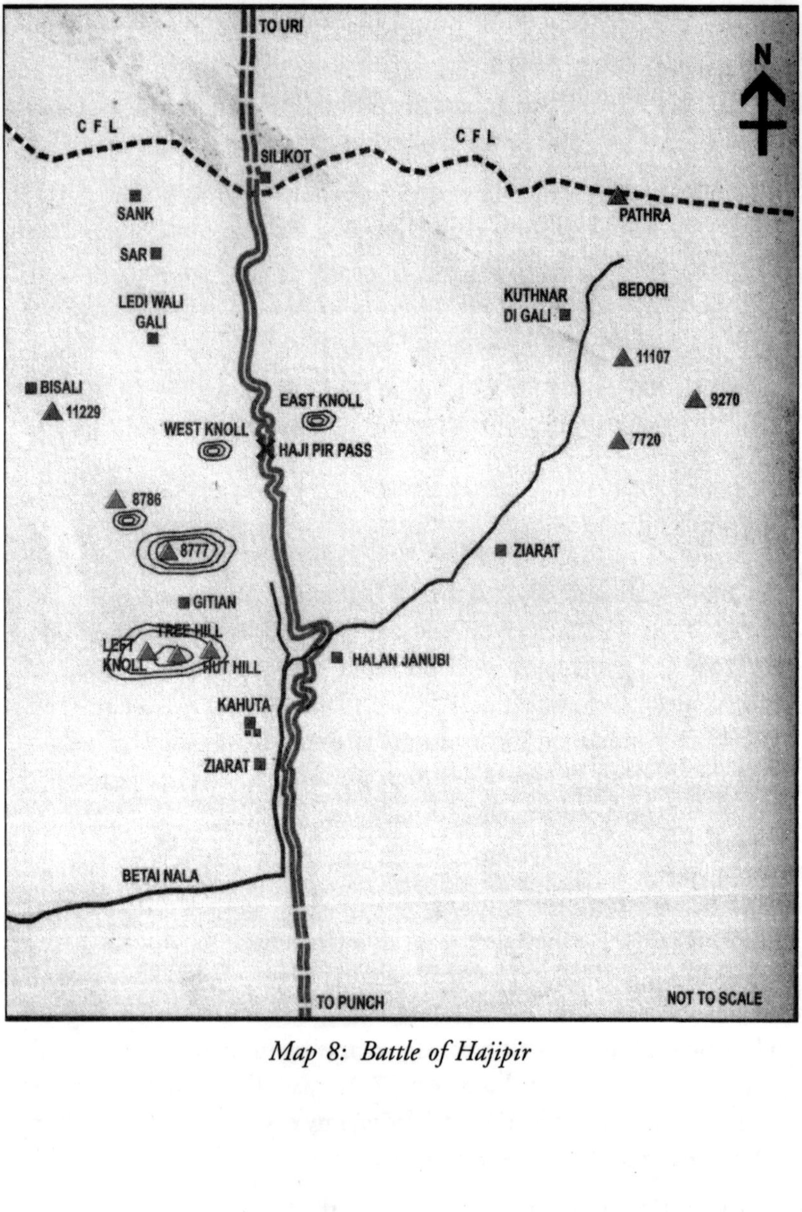

Map 8: Battle of Hajipir

for permission to press on to the Hajipir Pass immediately with his company. The permission was granted. Major Dayal and his company accompanied by an artillery officer started at 1400 hours on 27 August. As they descended into the valley, they came under fire from the western shoulder of the pass. There were minor skirmishes with the enemy withdrawing from Sank. Towards evening a drizzle began and a thick mist enveloped the mountain. This made movement and direction keeping difficult. The men had already been in battle for almost two days and were quite exhausted. But Major Dayal urged them on.

On reaching the foot of the pass, Major Dayal decided to leave the track and climb straight up to surprise the enemy. He and his men climbed the difficult hillside by night carrying heavy loads through the rain, often wading through knee deep water. At 0430 hours they hit the Uri-Poonch road. They had a short break. By 0600 hours they had arrived at the foot of the Pass. They now came under fire from the enemy. Leaving the leading platoon and the artillery officer to engage the enemy, Major Dayal took the rest of his men to the right, climbed the western shoulder of the Pass and then rolled down on the enemy from a flank. The Pakistanis were completely surprised. They left their weapons and ran down the hill and escaped. Thus 1 PARA captured the Pass by 1030 hours on 28 August.

The enemy brigade was stung by this loss and counter attacked on 29 August. 1 PARA repulsed the counter attack and over the next two days captured a few other features and consolidated their position. They held firm till the cease-fire. Major Ranjit Singh Dayal was awarded the Maha Vir Chakra for his gallantry and leadership in the battle.

The eastern thrust required to converge on Hajipir got stalled. 19 PUNJAB also commenced operations on the night of 26 August. It captured Pathra but got stalled at Bedori, a strongly held feature. An attempt by 4 RAJPUT from the north also failed. 19 PUNJAB attacked again the next night and captured the feature by evening of

28 August. 4 RAJPUT, the third battalion of the brigade captured Bisali, an enemy position west of Hajipir on 5 September. The enemy counter attacked Bisali and succeeded in recapturing it. The Rajputs fell back on Sank. The link up with 93 Infantry Brigade took place on 10 September. The entire Hajipir bulge was thus captured by Indian troops.

Analysis

The capture of Hajipir Pass by 1 PARA was a remarkable achievement. The Battalion not only captured the objectives allotted to it in the Phase 1 of the Brigade attack but also the task allotted to 4 RAJPUT in Phase 2 of the Brigade attack. It is perhaps relevant to examine how this was possible.

Achievement of surprise. A silent attack in difficult terrain in most adverse weather conditions caught the enemy defending Sank by surprise. They did not expect a major attack and were literally caught sleeping. Even the enemy troops defending the Pass were surprised by the speed of movement of the Indian troops and assault from an unexpected direction and fled without offering a determined fight.

Ability of the Battalion to exploit success. A defeated enemy requires time to regroup, reorganise and put up a fight. 1 PARA gave the enemy no time to reorganise and put up a fight after the loss of Sank. Their relentless offensive action without the classical reorganisation after a battle, kept the enemy off balance. The enemy could not mount a coordinated counter attack till 29 September. By then the Indian troops had been able to consolidate their position and were able to beat back the counter attack.

Leadership. The leadership of Brigadier Bakshi and Major Dayal was outstanding. Their gallantry and personal example inspired their men to perform great feats of bravery and endurance and achieve what was considered impossible.

THE FIRST BATTLE OF DOGRAI

15 Infantry Division was allotted the task to "secure Pakistan territory up to the east bank of the Ichhogil Canal from Ichhogil Canal-Ravi river junction (inclusive) to the Canal-track crossing 4 kilometres south of Jallo (inclusive)". It was to capture and hold the bridges over the Ichhogil Canal on the GT Road, Ichhogil Uttar and Jallo.

Major General Niranjan Prasad, GOC 15 Infantry Division, appreciated that the main enemy defences were based on the Ichhogil Canal, which had been specially developed as a strong obstacle, and the covering positions of the main Pakistani defences were in the Gosal Dial area, manned by an infantry battalion and strong elements of supporting arms. Between the International Border and Gosal Dial, there were various Pak police and para-military forces manning the Wagah Check-post and a series of border posts. He suggested that the international border should be crossed immediately after last light, and not at first light, so that his troops could dig in on the eastern bank of the Ichhogil Canal during the hours of darkness. But the Corps Commander did not agree to this to achieve surprise along the whole front simultaneously.

General Prasad made the following operational plan:

(a) 1 JAT (From 38 Infantry Brigade) with under command one troop of Sherman tanks of Scinde Horse to capture the bridge Bhaini-Malakapur.

(b) 54 Infantry Brigade, under the command of Brigadier M.S. Rikh, to advance on the GT Road axis, clear Gosal Dial and establish a firm base; and subsequently, capture the main road and rail bridges over the Ichhogil canal.

(c) 38 Brigade, commanded by Brigadier P.W. Pathak, less one battalion—1 JAT, under immediate Divisional control, to act as reserve for 54 Infantry Brigade operations.

Phase I of the operation was to be carried out by 54 Infantry Brigade and 1 JAT Group, commanded by Lt Col Balbir Singh. 54 Infantry Brigade had under its command 13 PUNJAB, 3 JAT and

15 DOGRA, commanded by Lieutenant Colonel H. Chatterjee, Lieutenant Colonel D. E. Hayde and Lieutenant Colonel Inderjit Singh respectively. 54 Infantry Brigade and 1 JAT Group crossed the Indo-Pak border at 0400 hrs on 6 September 1965 on the Grand Trunk Road axis and on Ichhogil Uttar axis respectively.

The Plan of 54 Infantry Brigade was an advance by 3 JAT cross-country and the capture of Gosal Dial as the first bound. 15 Dogra were to clear the road axis by destroying any enemy opposition at Wagah and between Wagah and Gosal Dial, and blow up the steel gates at the border check post. 13 PUNJAB commando platoon was detailed to advance simultaneously along Wagah Distributary in a bid to capture the Jallo bridge over the Ichhogil Canal. After the capture of Gosal Dial by 3 JAT, 15 DOGRA were to pass through and secure east bank of Ichhogil canal, including Grand Trunk Road bridge, if intact.

Initial Successes

After crossing the International Border, 3 JAT attacked the objective astride mile 14 on the Amritsar-Lahore road and captured it by 0630 hours. Village Dial was also cleared at 0658 hours.

At 0700 hours, Pakistani aircraft carried out intensive rocketing and bombing on 3 JAT and 15 DOGRA positions. Later, Pakistani Sabres attacked several places on the Grand Trunk Road, including Gharenda, where the Divisional Commander had his command post and the Divisional reserves. The air attacks were pressed home with determination, and they took a heavy toll of vehicles. With the skies all to themselves, the PAF had no difficulty in picking out any vehicle which moved. Several ammunition trucks were hit, and the ammunition kept exploding for hours, obstructing the road, which in turn made it necessary to make detours through slushy rice fields. Almost the entire 'F' echelon vehicles of 54 Infantry Brigade were destroyed. 3 JAT lost its 2nd-in-Command, besides 5 of 6 RCL guns, and 3 mortars with their carriers.

During capture of Gosal Dial, 3 JAT killed 35 enemy troops and captured 2 Officers and 12 Other Ranks, along with 2x106 RCL guns, 3 mounted Jeeps, 3 trucks and 45 weapons. The battalion was then ordered to continue its advance towards Ichhogil Canal, which commenced at 0900 hours. The east bank of Ichhogil Canal, about 1,280 metres north of the GT road, was assaulted and captured. 3 JAT also captured vital GT Road Bridge over the canal at 1130 hours and tried to consolidate their position. Although the bridge had been demolished by the enemy, 3 JAT could scamper over the surviving portions of macadam and masonry. The Pakistanis, however, reacted at once. They attacked 3 JAT, first with two 8-ton truck-loads of soldiers and shortly after with three tanks and about 100 infantry in support. However, both these attacks were repulsed, and the enemy withdrew. Soon, a squadron of Pakistani Sherman tanks advanced south along the west bank of the canal. Due to the lack of anti-tank weapons, Indian troops withdrew to east bank. It was only after the arrival of 14 Horse in support that A and B Company's and CO's party again crossed over to west bank, and a series of tank-to-tank fights took place. 'C' Coy reached Batapore complex and fought against the enemy. Requests for immediate reinforcement of anti-tank weapons were repeatedly sent, while the Pakistanis continued intense shelling of the Indian positions.

By the afternoon, 3 JAT had expended most of their ammunition. At about 1420 hours, the unit was ordered by the Brigade Commander to withdraw to the firm base of 15 Dogra (Gosal Dial). During the action, 3 JAT's losses were 9 killed and 43 wounded. Hayde was wounded and awarded MVC, and Subedar Khazan Singh received a Vir Chakra.

15 DOGRA also crossed the International Border at 0400 hours to clear the Ranger Posts and the bridge. They attacked a weak company of the Pakistani regular army on the Upper Bari Doab Canal (UBDC) bridge and occupied it. Advancing further they attacked the Ranger Posts successfully and captured 20 PsOW, including one Officer, along with arms, ammunition and vehicles. The unit lost one Officer and 13 ORs killed, and one Officer, 2 JCOs and 16 ORs wounded in this action. According to the plan,

the battalion was to move forward with C Squadron 14 HORSE to clear the main axis and press on to the GT road bridge over the Ichhogil Canal. But an exaggerated account of the casualties suffered by the unit was reported to the Brigade Commander. Consequently, the original plan was modified and the task of capturing the GT road bridge was entrusted to 3 JAT, while 15 Dogra was ordered to firm in at Dial.

13 PUNJAB commando platoon also advanced towards Jallo bridge, and despite enemy fire from the area 550 metres west of Wagah, went forward astride the railway track up to about 450 metres of the Rail bridge. Here they were subjected to heavy shelling and air attacks, forcing them to withdraw to Wagah Railway Station. On the other hand, 1 JAT Group after crossing the Indo-Pak border was fired upon from the Pakistani police post at Ichhogil Hithar. The resistance was, however, overcome, and the Pak Ranger Post at Ichhogil Hithar as well as the Ichhogil Uttar bridge were captured by 0700 hours. Reserve companies and tanks had also advanced for the operation, but were halted due to intensive Pakistani artillery shelling and air strafing. As no support was forthcoming from the Indian artillery, armour or air, the battalion withdrew to Ranian Bund, and reorganised. As the men of this unit had not taken their digging tools with them, they could not hold the ground. During this action, the unit suffered casualties of 13 ORs killed, and one Officer and 28 ORs injured.

THE SECOND BATTLE OF DOGRAI

On 12 September, Brigadier Niranjan Singh, MC, had taken over command of 54 Infantry Brigade. 54 Infantry Brigade was ordered to plan for advance up to the Ichhogil Canal astride Grand Trunk road which involved the capture of Dograi. It was believed that the main Pakistani defences were along the Ichhogil Canal and Dograi, with a screen along the general line Jhuggian Main-Daraswali–Lakhanke, supported by armour along Pul Distributary and astride UBDC on the flanks.

The planning and preparations including domination of no-man's-land, collection of information, surprise and deception measures, development of tracks and other administrative arrangements connected with the stage management of the battle, preliminary operations, issue of orders, and redeployment of troops for attack, were carried out between 13 and 20 September. During this period, the Brigade suffered 58 killed, including 3 Officers and 4 JCOs, and 205 wounded, including 5 Officers and 7 JCOs.

From information extracted during the interrogation of two Pakistani Prisoners of War, captured on night 14/15 September, it was known that the disposition of Pak forces was:

(a) Two companies 16 PUNJAB (Pathan) astride the bridge SB 745114.

(b) Mortar platoon west of the house at SB 743114.

(c) Battalion Headquarters battalion and remainder battalion at Dograi.

(d) Company 15 Frontier Force Rifles deployed astride the Grand Trunk road, and

(e) Squadron of tanks in Dograi.

Final orders for the operation were issued on 20 September at 1700 hours. The attack was to be launched in two phases. In Phase I, 13 PUNJAB was to attack on area Mile 13 at 2359 hours on 21 September, and in Phase II, 3 JAT was to attack Dograi itself at 0130 hours on 22 September.

Phase I: Attack by 13 PUNJAB

On 19 September, 13 PUNJAB had relieved 15 DOGRA in area Dial and Jhuggian Mian Daraswali, and was ordered to capture area Mile 13 from the direction of Lakhanke. On 21 September, it was ordered that the area Mile 13 was to be captured in Phase I with D company on left and C company on right, astride the road, from Jhuggian. A company from Lakhanke on relief by a platoon of 15

DOGRA rejoined the battalion at 2100 hours on 21 September, and was approximately 180 metres ahead of Jhuggian. 'H' hour was at 2359 hours 21 September, and the objective was to be captured by 0130 hours 22 September. Artillery and brigade mortars were to shell Mile 13 position from H minus 10 to H plus 4 minutes.

At about 2200 hours, a threat of a Pakistani attack developed on D company, located south of Jhuggian. The enemy, approximately platoon strength, supported by BMG and mortar fire, tried to close in. This enemy action, which might have been intended as a spoiling attack, was beaten back by D company.

The Indian attack was delayed, and was launched at 0100 hours on 22 September due to heavy enemy shelling during forming up. The attack was supported by a squadron of tanks from area south of Jhuggian, brigade mortars north of GT road, Bren guns of 15 DOGRA, south of GT road, and Divisional Artillery. In spite of heavy enemy shelling, which had commenced right from 2200 hours, D and C companies formed up astride the GT road and carried out the assault. When they were approximately 180 metres from the frontline of the enemy defences, they were pinned down by intensive MMG, Mortar and arty fire from all directions. In spite of the heavy casualties suffered (1 Officer and 24 ORs killed, and 4 Officers 5 JCOs and 83 ORs wounded), both these companies did not leave the ground they had occupied. Soon after first light, the assault was resumed on either side of GT Road axis, with tanks moving along with both these companies giving support to each other. As a result of this infantry/tank advance, the enemy left their trenches and ran towards village Dograi. The objective was captured at about 0700 hours after inflicting heavy casualties on the enemy on the ground and on those fleeing toward s Dograi. This operation was a great success and positive contributions were made by 13 PUNJAB. By containing the bulk of the enemy on the main GT Road axis, they facilitated the task of the capture of Dograi by 3 JAT. By dislodging the enemy from Mile 13 area, they also provided security to 3 JAT; made possible 3 JAT's capture of a large number of prisoners as well as a large booty of enemy arms, ammunition and equipment; and opened the maintenance of the GT Road axis up to the Ichhogil Canal.

The battalion captured a number of weapons and ammunition including recoilless guns, MGs, mortars and other small arms. It suffered 31 killed, including one Officer and 5 JCOs, and over a hundred wounded, including 5 Officers and 5 JCOs, during the attack. The enemy casualties were 15 counted killed and 3 Prisoners, of War.

Phase II: Attack by 3 JAT

Since early morning, 21 September, all ranks of 3 JAT had gone on patrol many times to have a look at Dograi which was to be attacked that night. They found that the Pakistanis were well entrenched, "some huddled over machine guns in pill-boxes and others tucked into the buildings of Dograi behind light machine guns and rifles, with piles of ammunition and grenades to hand". With two light machine guns in each infantry section, "their automatic fire was going to spew forth from every 30 to 50 yards of front while artillery and mortar shells rained down". 3 JAT were to run through minefields, jump over or cut their way through wire entanglements and penetrate bullets and shells and only then to contact the enemy. The FUP was just 400 metres from the nearest enemy trench, and to reach it, 3 JAT (523 men) had to pass through the minefields in a single file. Taking the Pakistani defences into account, the battalion prepared its plan to attack the township of Dograi, which extended for 1,100 metres from north to south along the Ichhogil Canal, and 760 metres from east to west across the GT road, by infiltration from the north. The town was guarded by reinforced concrete pill-boxes around its three approaches. The built-up area had been divided into four sectors as company objectives.

A company less one platoon secured the north-east flank of the battalion and the forming-up-place in area Ruins (SB 7412). The battalion moved from Santpura at 2330 hours on 21 September, and reached its firm base north of Lakhanke at 0045 hours the next

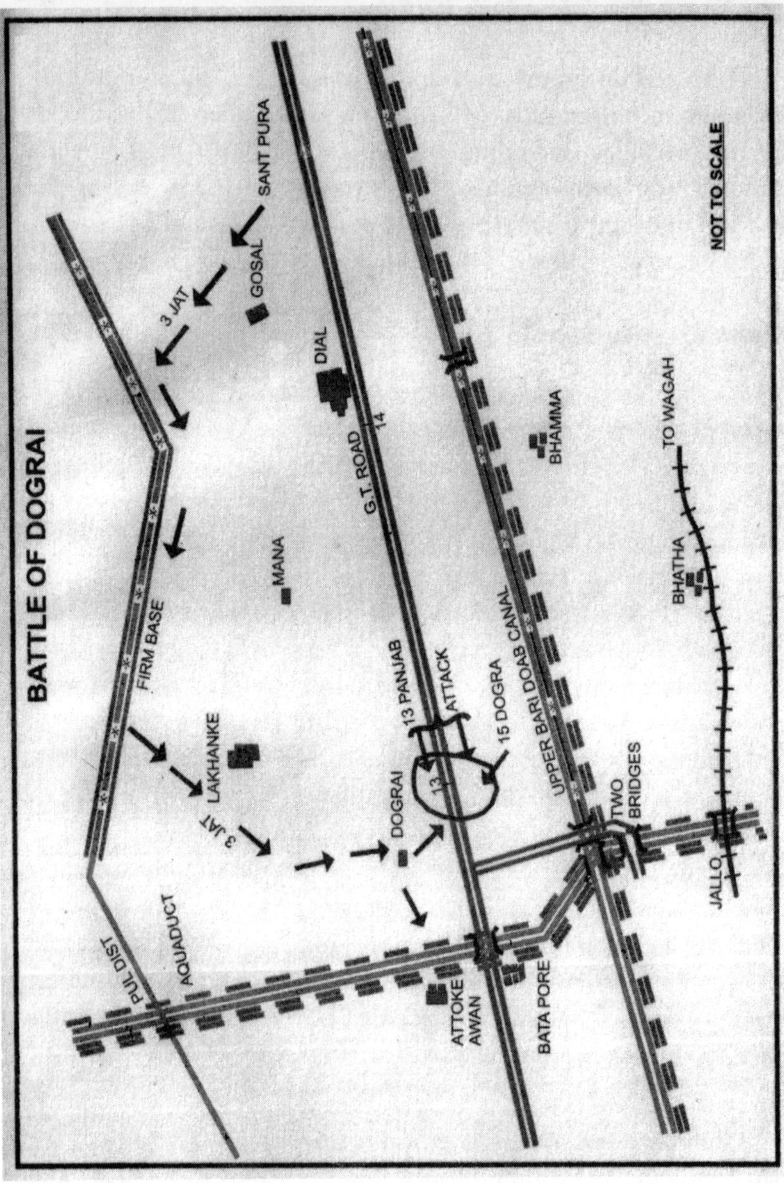

Map 9: Battle of Dograi

day, after a march of 3,700 metres. After a short rest, the battalion left the firm base at 0110 hours and moved from the PUL Distributary into the forming-up-place.

The leading company (D company under Major Vatsa) crossed the start line at 0150 hours on 22 September, and after fighting through the outskirts of the town and silencing a pill-box enroute, secured the north-east projection of the town against minor opposition.

C company, under Major Yadav, passed through D company to secure the north-west portion of Dograi. Suddenly, it was subjected to very intense fire and got engaged in a fierce battle with a company of 18 Baluch, entrenched in pill-boxes along the east bank of the Ichhogil Canal in the Akbar School area, north of Dograi. The company charged the bank undaunted by the enemy's protective mine-field. Grenade and hand-to-hand fighting took place inside the enemy company-defended-locality, during which a platoon commander, Lieutenant Thapa of D company, was killed. The price paid by 3 JAT was heavy, the survivors were only one officer and 7 men, but the enemy company was wiped out. The depth platoon of C Company under Captain Bali was not drawn off into this assault. It attacked and captured the north-west projection of the town, which was actually the company's objective. Thus the gate to Dograi from the north-west had been opened wide.

B Company under Major Sandhu cut through the centre of Dograi to secure the south-west portion of the town. They silenced a pill-box on the junction of GT road and Ichhogil Canal, and fought a platoon of 3 Baluch, entrenched on the eastern bank of the Ichhogil Canal.

A company, under Major Tyagi, passed along the eastern edge of Dograi, where D company was still fighting, on to the southern edge of the town. The company silenced a MG in a pill-box on the GT road, and fighting across the road, took the surrender of a troop of 23 Cavalry, and the remnants of 16 PUNJAB and the brigade mortars, nine of which were in perfect order and five in damaged condition. This company came under very intense automatic fire of a company of 8 PUNJAB, entrenched along a pill-box guarding the southern approach to Dograi. The men of A company fought a very gallant action under the inspiring leadership of Maj Asha Ram Tyagi, who was mortally wounded.

The battalion secured the objective by 0530 hours on 22 September. A number of enemy pockets in Dograi still remained to be cleared. The houses along both sides of the GT Road at the eastern edge of Dograi had developed into little enemy strongpoint's. A platoon was detailed to clear out these houses. It flushed out about a dozen men from a room, one of whom attempted to dive under a captured enemy tank, but was dragged out. The man was Lieutenant Colonel G.F. Golewala, Commanding Officer 16 PUNJAB. In the 27 incredible hours of non-stop combat, 3 JAT never paused to count or consider. The price paid by 3 JAT for the capture of Dograi was 58 killed, including 4 Officers, and 157 wounded, including 6 Officers and 4 JCOs.

Thus the operation launched by 54 Infantry Brigade was a complete success. Considerable amount of arms and equipment and over 108 prisoners, including the enemy battalion commander, were captured, and 300 Pak dead bodies were counted. The Battle of Dograi added a glorious chapter to the history of the Indian Army. Two officers were awarded the MVC, and 2 JCOs and one Sepoy won the Vir Chakra.

After this feat, 3 JAT was looking for the logistic support to hold on to the captured position. There was an urgent need for replenishment of ammunition and reorganisation of stores to secure the ground gained. But the battalion was neither reinforced, nor were supplies pushed. This was a serious administrative failure; which enabled a brilliant success to slip away unexploited. Air support for such a venture was essential, but it appears that the Corps Commander did not ask for it, although there was a demand for it from the Division. The result was that when the Pakistan Air Force was attacking Indian troops, guns and vehicles, there was no help forthcoming from the Indian Air Force. However, the ceasefire intervened to stop further action. According to Lieutenant General Harbakhsh Singh, the Dograi battle "will go down in history as one of the toughest ever fought".

BATTLE OF ASAL UTTAR

Background

4 Mountain Division was trained and organised to fight in the mountains and its normal operational role was on the northern border. In June 1965, GOC 4 Mountain Division was sounded that in the event of conflict with Pakistan, the division would be given an offensive task in 11 Corps sector. The division was ordered on 4 September to move for Operation Riddle.

In the 1950s, a huge pond existed near Kasur in which the Rohi Nala and Sutlej outflow entered. By 1965 the whole area had been drained off and a thick jungle grew there which had the ability to hide a concentration of armour which Indian aircraft could not detect. Pakistan had also constructed two big aqueducts on the Ichhogil Canal, one north and another south of Khem Karan which were used by the Pakistani armour to launch a two-pronged attack on 4 Mountain Division.

On 5/6 September, Indian 11 Corps launched its three divisions in offensives in the Lahore sector. 4 Mountain Division was on the southern axis, from Khem Karan towards Kasur, approximately 7 kilometres from the international border. The Pakistani formations defending the Lahore sector were their 10 and 11 Infantry Divisions. (There was no controlling Corps HQ).

4 Mountain Division (two brigades) and a Sherman regiment (9 HORSE) attacked, expecting to be opposed by a single regular infantry battalion. Instead, it found a brigade reinforced with armour, and the entire Pakistan 1 Armoured Division in the area of their planned offensive. 21 and 52 Infantry Brigades of the Pakistan 11 Infantry Division were defending Kasur. 11 Division, though a

completely new formation, was led by Major General Hamid, who showed a capacity for rapid action aimed at keeping the initiative.

Opposing Forces

India

4 Mountain Division (Major General Gurbaksh Singh)

9 (DECCAN) HORSE (Lieutenant Colonel A.S. Vaidya) Sherman IV/V

7 Mountain Brigade (Brigadier D.S. Sidhu)
- 4 GRENADIERS
- 7 GRENADIERS
- 9 JAK RIF

62 Mountain Brigade (Brigadier H.C. Gahlaut)
- 1/9 GR
- 13 DOGRA
- 18 RAJ RIF

2 (Independent) Armoured Brigade (Brigadier T.K. Theograj)
- 3 CAV (Lieutenant Colonel Salim Caleb) Centurions
- 8 CAV (Lieutenant Colonel P.C. Mehta) AMX-13
- 1 Field Regiment (SP) (Sextons)

Pakistan

1 Armoured Division (Major General Nasir Ahmed)

3 Armoured Brigade (Brigadier Moen)
- 19 LANCERS
- 7 FF
- 16 Field Regiment (SP)

4 Armoured Brigade (Brigadier Lumb)
- 4 CAVALRY
- 5 HORSE
- 10 FF
- 15 Field Regiment (SP)

5 Armoured Brigade (Brigadier Bashir Ahmad)
6 LANCERS
24 CAVALRY
1 FF
3 Field Regiment (SP)

21 Medium Regiment
19 LAA Regiment (SP)

11 Infantry Division (Major General Hamid)
15 LANCERS
32 TDU

21 Infantry Brigade (Brigadier Sahib Dad)
5 FF
13 BALUCH

52 Infantry Brigade (Brigadier S.R.H. Rizvi)
7 PUNJAB
12 BALUCH
2 FF

196 Infantry Brigade (Brigadier Nawazish Ali)
7 BALUCH
1 EAST BENGAL

Plan

4 Mountain Division planned its offensive in two phases. In the first phase, Pakistani territory up to the east bank of Ichhogil Canal from Ballanwala to Point RO 798489 was to be captured by 62 Mountain Brigade Group. In the second phase, Pak territory east of Ichhogil Canal from Canal Junction RO 763767 to Ballanwala was to be captured by 7 Mountain Brigade Group less a battalion. The offensive was ordered by HQ 11 Corps at 0330 hours on 6 September.

Before the offensive commenced, a firm base had been established by 4 Mountain Division in an area southwest of Khemkaran, consisting of 1/9 GR, 18 RAJ RIF and 9 HORSE less two squadrons, under 62 Mountain Brigade Group. This compact defended sector covered the axes Kasur-Khem Karan and Gandasinghwala-Khem Karan.

The offensive commenced at 0500 hours on 6 September. According to the intelligence available, Pakistan had only Sutlej Rangers and Mujahid posts east of the Ichhogil Canal and, at the most one infantry battalion in hastily prepared positions, deployed from Bedian to Point RO 798439. No firm information of the location of the Pakistani 1 Armoured Division was available. Consequently, the time when the enemy would launch his offensive with 1 Armoured Division and an infantry division (two brigades) was not foreseen, and quick Pakistani reaction was not expected.

In view of the quantum of resistance visualised, it was thought that initial occupation of the east bank of the Rohi Nala would delay enemy armour thrusts, enable the Indians to cause more attrition and economise troop involvement to defend the likely axes of the enemy advance.

Initial Operations

62 Mountain Brigade advanced to secure area Rohiwal and the road crossing over Rohi Nala. 9 JAK RIF reported capture of Rohi Nala on the main axis at about 0915 hours. It was then directed to continue with its task to push through and destroy the bridge on the Ichhogil Canal and occupy its near bank. However, the unit came under heavy artillery and MMG fire from the enemy on the Ichhogil Canal. 13 DOGRA also succeeded in securing area Rohiwal by 1030 hours, although it was under mortar and MMG fire from the enemy and suffered some casualties, including two officers.

Two battalions of 7 Mountain Brigade, 7 GRENADIERS and 4 GRENADIERS, also advanced towards Ballanwala and Theh

Pannun respectively. By 1130 hours on 6 September, these battalions secured the line of Rohi Nala and east bank of Ichhogil Canal from Theh Pannun southwards, except Ballanwala, where the 7 GRENADIERS attack had failed, because Ballanwala was a stronghold of the Pakistani defences.

Pakistan reacted quickly with Patton tanks and motorised infantry. At 1530 hours on 6 September, 13 DOGRA came under heavy artillery fire prior to a counterattack by one Pakistani battalion-cum-armour squadron group. 13 DOGRA had to abandon its position. Throughout the night 6/7 September, all defended localities and gun areas were subjected to very heavy, accurate and sustained artillery fire. By first light 7 GRENADIERS also had to withdraw. At about 0700 hours, the 9 JAK RIF position was encircled by Pakistani tanks and strafed by the enemy aircraft. They could extricate with assistance of the tanks of 9 HORSE.

By then, the enemy's violent reaction to the Indian move in this sector foretold his major offensive design. The enemy advanced with tanks and motorised infantry not along the expected axes, but from flanks through Patto Kuhna and Ballanwala and threatened to bypass the firm base. By 0800 hours on 7 September it was realised that a strong Pakistani armoured thrust towards axis Khem Karan-Bhikiwind from the north of road Khem Karan-Kasur was imminent and that the defended sector occupied in the area west and south-west of Khem Karan would be bypassed. Accordingly, it was decided to fall back and occupy a defended sector north of Khem Karan to cover the axes Khem Karan-Patti and Khem Karan-Bhikiwind in the general area of Asal Uttar-Bhura Kuhna-Chima, and 7 Mountain Brigade, which had captured area Theh Pannun and linked up with Bedian, was ordered to fall back on the defended sector.

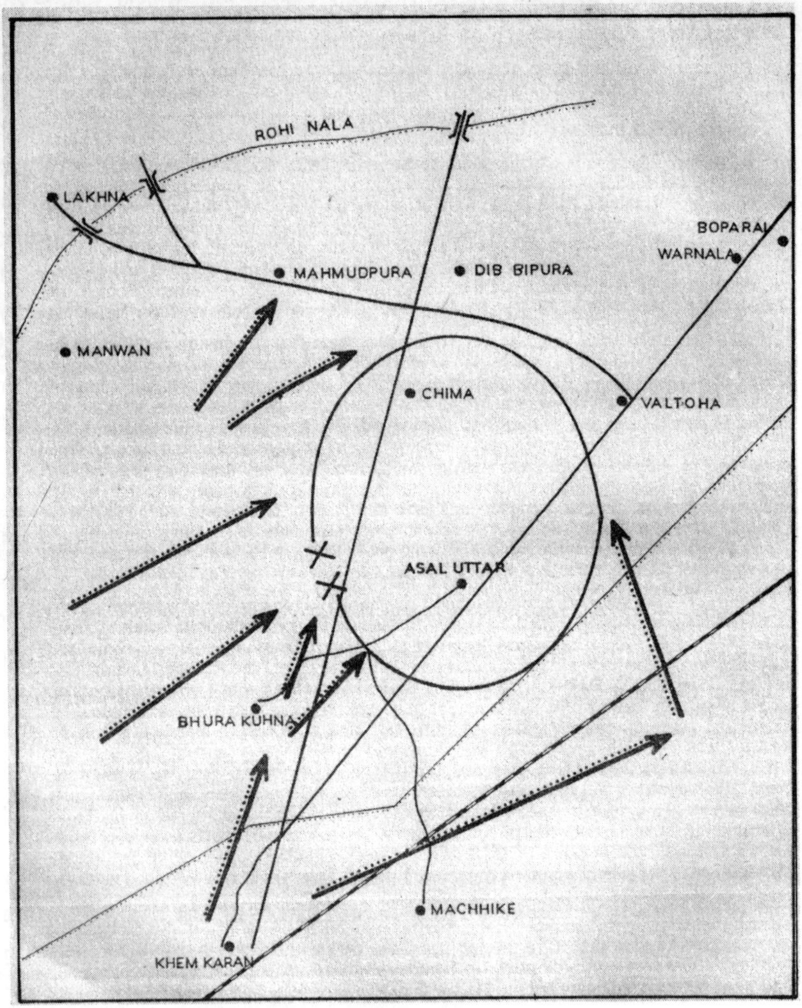

Map 10: Battle of Asal Uttar

By last light 7 September, defences were occupied as under:

18 RAJ RIF	Area south of Asal Uttar covering the axis Khem Karan-Patti
1/9 GR	Area Road-track junction, covering the axis Khem Karan-Bhikiwind
4 GRENADIERS	Area south of Chima covering axis Khem Karan-Bhikiwind to give depth to 1/9 GR positions
9 J&K RIF (Two companies)	Area north of Asal Uttar giving depth to 18 RAJ RIF location

9 HORSE with a company of 1/9 GR, to cover the preparation of defences, were deployed in area southwest of Khem Karan.

The Pakistani Offensive

Pakistan's plan was to establish a lodgement area with 11 Infantry Division, with under command 5 Armoured Brigade, up to the general line running east to west of Bhura Kuhna village. Concurrently, 1 Armoured Division with under command 4 Armoured Brigade was to advance along road Valtoha-Patti to secure Raya and the GT road bridge on River Beas. 3 Armoured Brigade, under the command of 1 Armoured Division, was to advance on road Khem Karan-Bhikiwind to secure Jandialaguru. The further role assigned to 5 Armoured Brigade was to revert to its parent formation and to advance to Road Khem Karan-Bhikhiwind to protect the left flank of the forward two combat groups and to cut the rear of Indian 7 Infantry Division, operating on road Bhikiwind-Khalra-Barki. The Pakistani plan was to occupy Harike bridge by 8 September and to secure Beas and other objectives by 9-10 September. It avoided the crossing of any water obstacle and aimed at capturing Indian territory west of River Beas and encircling 11 Indian Corps. If it succeeded, it would have brought the Pakistan Army quick and spectacular success.

Considering the situation, Major General Gurbaksh Singh, GOC

Indian 4 Mountain Division immediately ordered the division to fall back and assume a horseshoe-shaped defensive position with Asal Uttar as its focal point. This village had a population of about 1,500. Asal Uttar was chosen because it was located at the focal point of two roads leading from Pakistan to Khem Karan, and thus the defenders could cover both likely axes of advance.

At 0930 hours on 8 September, approximately two squadrons of Chaffees approached 4 Mountain Division position through Ballanwala as a reconnaissance in force. Approaching on a broad front, they surrounded Indian defended localities, and from their right flank sallied up to the gun area. In the ensuing action, the Pakistani's lost two Chaffees and withdrew. Meanwhile, work on the preparation of defences was progressing. By the afternoon of 8 September, three and a half battalions of Indian troops had dug the defences around Asal Uttar and laid some mines.

Again at 1445 hours, the Pakistanis carried out a reconnaissance in force with a regiment of Pattons. They overran the position of 1/ 9 GR. 9 HORSE now played an important role in stopping the enemy in front of the Indian defended sector. A diversionary attack by Pattons fell on 4 GRENADIERS and the gun area, but it was halted in area Rattoke. Pakistani troops again tried to bypass the defended sector on the north, but a squadron of 3 CAV in area Bhikhiwind had anticipated this move and was ready to receive it. It moved down immediately and attacked the enemy, inflicting heavy casualties and forcing it to withdraw.

After this reconnaissance in force by the enemy, it became evident that a major armoured thrust was likely to take place next day. At 0200 hours, on 9 September the Pakistani 4 Armoured Brigade (with two Patton regiments), making use of moonlight and infra-red equipment, attacked 18 RAJ RIF. The Indian artillery and infantry engaged the enemy with concentrations and recoilless guns. Although the enemy tanks had a free and uninterrupted run, they failed to dislodge the Indian defences. What appeared to be desperate Indian situation was thus saved.

At 0430 hrs on 9 September, 2 (Independent) Armoured Brigade was placed in support of 4 Mountain Division, and moved from its concentration area. 3 CAV less a squadron and 8 CAV less a squadron moved without incident and the defences were strengthened by laying more mines.

Orders were issued that the Indian armour would operate at night, and 9 HORSE would stay in the forward defended localities and gun area in an anti-tank role. The deployment in 4 Mountain Division sector in the morning of 9 September was:

(a) 62 Brigade defended sector consisting of three and a half battalions in the Asal Uttar area with 9 HORSE less a squadron.

(b) One squadron 9 HORSE protecting the gun areas and deployed between the brigade defended sector and the gun area.

(c) 3 CAV less two troops between Dibbipura and Chima.

(d) One squadron 8 CAV east of Valtoha to protect the southern flank.

(e) 8 CAV less two squadrons in the area Warnala in depth.

Pakistan's attempt to over-run 4 GRENADIERS during early hours on 9 September had already failed. It then made another attempt during the night to overrun 18 RAJ RIF positions. However, the battalion was told to hold fast, and the enemy was taken on by medium artillery and tanks, located in forward defended localities. At 0330 hours, the enemy infantry, in armoured personnel carriers, probed forward, but, on hitting the mine-field, withdrew, and a lull followed. Pakistan carried out reconnaissance in force with tanks throughout the latter part of night 9/10 September.

The final enemy attack came at 0645 hours on 10 September. Pakistani tanks concentrated in area Manawan, with a view to bypassing the Indian defended sector. At 0830 hrs, a Pakistani combat group from 4 Armoured Brigade was launched against 4 GRENADIERS, but the attack was foiled by artillery concentration before the enemy infantry could close on to the Indian minefield. Indian armour then came from the flank, resulting in a tank melee. Here, a recoilless gun manned by Havildar Abdul Hamid knocked out 3 Patton tanks, and he posthumously got the first Param Vir Chakra in the Division during this war.

By now, Indian 2 Armoured Brigade with two regiments (one Centurion, one AMX-13) had moved to reinforce Indian 4 Mountain Division. On the 8 and 9 September, Pakistan armour attacked repeatedly, to be beaten back with heavy losses, both to the Indians and the terrain, which was soft in many places. On 10 September, the day of the last attack, the advancing Pakistani tanks ran into 4 Division's horseshoe ambush, and the attackers were annihilated. The ambush was placed in sugarcane fields—the crop was standing tall and ready to be harvested—and Indian Shermans had learned by now to hold their fire till Pakistani tanks came within 550-750 metres. At longer ranges Indian shells simply bounced off the Pattons. This ambush was only one part of the reason for the Pakistani defeat at Asal Uttar.

An outflanking move towards Mahmoodpura-Dibbipura by Pakistani 4 CAV (Pattons M-47) was then noticed. This was shadowed by Indian 3 CAV hinging on the defended sector. The Pakistani tanks were finally trapped in the area Mahmoodpura. It was at 1430 hours that GOC Pakistani 1 Armoured Division, Major General Nasir Ahmed, who had earlier witnessed the battle from a helicopter, came with his 'R' group to area Mile 37 on road Khem Karan-Bhikhiwind to push the advance personally. The party was surprised by 4 GRENADIERS and a heavy artillery concentration, and the entire 'R' group was dissipated at about 1800 hours. After the destruction of two Pakistani combat groups, the offensive of the Pakistani 1 Armoured Division was effectively foiled.

The other reason was that the Pakistan Chief of General Staff himself arrived to push the offensive forward. He took over the business of giving orders to the brigades—three command levels down. To ensure the CGS's orders were executed, GOC 1 Armoured

Division ordered Pakistan 5 Armoured Brigade to drive back some kilometres for a meeting. The conversations were intercepted, and the Indians ambushed the GOC's convoy, an indication of how interspersed the two armies were and how fluid the battlefield. The artillery brigadier was killed, and though the GOC escaped, Pakistan 1 Armoured Division completely disintegrated.

If the twin setbacks of Asal Uttar and the ambush were insufficient, on the same day Pakistan GHQ ordered the division's third brigade to the Sialkot sector, where fierce tank battles were underway. The next day 1 Armoured Division was reorganised. Its 4 and 5 Brigades were given one tank regiment and one armoured infantry battalion each, and the division HQ plus 4 Armoured Brigade was sent north against the possibility of an Indian breakthrough at Sialkot.

However, it was confirmed only on the morning of 11 September that enemy advance had been finally held, when officers and men of Pakistani 4 CAV started surrendering. Thus the enemy's drive with a superior force of armour, i.e. five Patton regiments (4 CAV, 5 HORSE, 6 LANCERS, 19 LANCERS and 24 CAV)and one Chaffee regiment (12 CAV), directed to capture all territory west of river Beas, and cut the rear of 11 Corps, was frustrated. Instead, of reaching the Beas, the enemy went back to Kasur to lick his wounds having lost 97 tanks, including 72 Pattons.

4 Mountain Division suffered casualties of 60 killed, 206 wounded, 93 missing, and lost 10 tanks. 2 (Independent) Armoured Brigade suffered one OR killed and 2 tanks lost.

Assessment

The Pakistani plans were to seize Khem Karan, opening the way for a rapid advance to the Beas River. The Beas had two bridges over it at this time and the Pakistani was to seize one bridge and then turn north. If successful, this manoeuvre would have isolated Indian 11 Corps. The Pakistani counterattack caught advanced Indian troops in a difficult position. They had pushed forward under the impression they faced only one regular infantry battalion supported by paramilitary forces, and were without reserves to sustain their offensive. They also had only one regiment of Sherman tanks which were no match for the Pakistan M47/48 Patton. Pakistan artillery had 140 guns available to the sector by pooling all units within range. The Indian 4 Mountain Division had 120mm mortars and 105mm pack howitzers, though a single heavy regiment was deployed in support. 106mm RCLs were deployed on a meagre scale of six per infantry battalion and were deemed to be ineffective against the Pakistani tanks except at close range. The PAF supported the ground troops with all means at its disposal.

Faced with imminent enemy onslaught, Commander 4 Mountain Division undertook useful defence preparations from the afternoon of 7 September to the forenoon of the next day. This was made possible by 2 companies of 9 JAK RIF and a squadron of 9 HORSE holding on the Rohi Nala and preventing the enemy from using the main axis till the evening of 7 September. In this, a good contribution was made by 14 Medium Regiment, which, despite orders to withdraw, made a continuous bombardment of Kasur, disrupting the enemy build-up.

On 7 September, Pakistan 11 Division established a bridgehead in Indian territory. Thereafter, Pakistan 5 Armoured Brigade of its 1 Armoured Division began the first Pakistani attack that culminated in the battle of Asal Uttar. Also concentrating in the bridgehead were 4 Armoured Brigade and 21 Infantry Brigade. It is difficult to tell how many attacks the Pakistanis made: 4 and 5 Armoured Brigades made at least five, perhaps seven or even eight attacks between them. At the very first, Pakistan 5 Brigade overran Khem Karan. Subsequently, however, every attack was defeated by the Indians though they did not succeed till after the ceasefire in getting back lost ground. Even Khem Karan, however, was not fully under Pakistan control till 10 September.

Also the quick move of 2 (Independent) Armoured Brigade to this sector on night 8/9 September prevented bypassing of the Indian defences by the Pakistani armour. Besides, the high standing sugar cane crops on the ground neutralised the superior range of the Patton's gun, restricting it to about 800 metres only. The gallantry of 4 GRENADIERS, 18 RAJ RIF and 9 JAK RIF, and good fire support provided by the artillery, jointly saved the situation.

The decisive victory at Asal Uttar aborted the ambitious Pakistani bid to penetrate deep into Indian territory. The mighty 1 Armoured Division of Pakistan was humbled and the Patton tanks invincibility was falsified. However, 4 Mountain Division's abortive attempt to recapture Khem Karan was an anti-climax to the brilliant performance at Asal Uttar. The plans were generally poor in conception; the troops were fed piecemeal to tasks that required well-coordinated action in strength, and attacks were launched in a hurry with inadequate preparation. Leadership at the brigade and battalion levels also left much to be desired in a number of cases. Thus the later operations were a series of disappointing failures.

Analysing the reasons of 4 Mountain Division defensive success against Pakistan in this sector, the Pakistanis followed the US method of offense without having a firm base, while the British method was to have a firm base first and then move forward. This led to the Pakistani debacle. 4 Mountain Division had planned and executed its defensive battle properly and luck also favoured the Division. The Pak counter-offensive in Khem Karan area with only armour but no infantry was a lucky break for him.

Pakistani Analysis

In 1965, Pakistan had two armoured divisions, 1 and 6. Both fought major battles. While 6 Armoured Division acquitted itself well, 1 Armoured Division failed miserably and completely. Its division commander, two of its three brigade commanders, and most of its staff officers were transferred out as reprimands for their unacceptable performance. This division witnessed scenes that have never taken place in the history of the Pakistan cavalry, before or since. We have an armoured regiment where, after the CO is killed, the 2nd-in-command refuses to take charge and none of the squadron commanders picks up when the 2nd-in-command refuses. We have armoured infantry abandoning their APCs when they come under friendly fire, and then running from the field, all the way back home. We have a regimental commander who achieves his phase line, but does not bother to inform his brigade, and then decides if the brigade—who has no idea where he is—does not link up with him that night, he will surrender in the morning. Seventy officers and men from two squadrons decide they had best push off while they can, and leave for Pakistani-held territory. The next morning, as good as his word, the regimental commander surrenders as soon as someone can be arranged to accept the surrender, and hands over 11 running tanks in the process. We have a divisional engineer regiment that builds a bridge across an obstacle, only to find the banks are too high for passage, and then has to rectify the problem, halting the entire division in the process. We have regimental commanders arguing with brigade commanders, brigade commanders arguing with the division commander, instead of cooperating to get on with the battle. We know all this and more because two Pakistani retired officers have written of these strange and perhaps unique events.

The Patton was a far superior tank to anything the Indians possessed, and the Pakistanis outnumbered the Indians 3-1 in tanks if we exclude Indian AMX-13s, and 3-0 in armoured infantry. The Patton had computers to handle firing solutions. Most important, it could fight at night, whereas none of the Indian tanks could. The Indians had perhaps half as many artillery pieces as the Pakistanis, and were outgunned to boot. The Pakistani artillery was absolutely first rate—a result of the excellent training imparted by the Americans. The Pakistanis had good air support, the IAF had its own problems and was usually absent. The pure infantry numbers were equal. Pakistani defences were long-planned and thickly constructed Indian defences were hastily thrown up in the field. The Pakistani commander had helicopters available to him, and could arrive anywhere on the battlefield in short order, and did. The Indian commander had no such advantage. So what went wrong?

(a) **Command failures at all levels.** According to Pakistani sources, GOC 1 Armoured Division, two brigade commanders, three of the six tank regimental commanders, all three of the infantry battalion commanders, and the engineer battalion commander failed to command their troops as required. The division was the pride of the Pakistan Army, and four of the six many of cavalry regiments plus all three Frontier Force Regiment infantry battalions were seasoned units with at least one hundred years of service each. How such a situation came about in a highly professional army and in the leading division of the Pakistan Army is not something outsiders can answer.

(b) **Dilution of cavalry regiments due to new raisings.** Under the 1954 US plan, Pakistan was to have eight tank regiments of 75 tanks each, and the US supplied approximately 700 tanks toward this end. This left ample numbers of tanks for war wastage and training. In 1962, Pakistan decided to switch to an establishment of 44 tanks per regiment this enabled 4 new regiments to be raised. Pakistan wanted to raise four more regiments, but this would have breached the manpower ceilings set by the US. Instead, Pakistan created four Tank Delivery Units, which in reality were reserve tank regiments. Between 1960 and 1965 Pakistan more than doubled the number of its armoured regiments, from 8 to 18, without increasing either its tank fleet or its training capabilities. India, by contrast, had yet to seriously undertake its armour expansion, so all its regiments were seasoned. Many of the Pakistani crews at Asall Uttar were inadequate trained because many tanks had 50 miles or less on their odometers, indicating they had been pulled straight from war reserves.

(c) **Role of infantry inadequately understood/7 Division shifted.** Pakistan seemed to have little conception that tanks require the close support of infantry. Time and again tanks were sent out with little or no infantry support, and on that fateful day at Asal Uttar, the tanks riding into the ambush had no infantry support. It is not as if infantry was short—the division had four battalions of its own and another battalion (1 FF) from 11 Division was under command.

(d) **No reconnaissance at Asal Uttar.** Pakistan sent its tanks to Asal Uttar without any reconnaissance. The Indians hid their Shermans in tall sugarcane fields—the crop was ready for harvesting. The Shermans were spaced out every 500 metres. When the Pakistanis rolled into the U-shaped Indian defensive positions, they were hit from every side while unable to see where the Indian fire was coming from. Though the Patton was almost invulnerable at range, at 6-800 meters it could be destroyed by Indian Centurions and Shermans. Moreover, the Patton tended to catch fire when hit, causing crews to bail out rapidly following a hit.

(e) **No logistics support.** The Pakistani tanks were lost after they ran out of fuel or got bogged down in soft terrain. Insufficient attention was paid to logistics to begin with and 1 Armoured Division was short of B vehicles. When the division moved for battle several hundred vehicles broke down because of insufficient peacetime maintenance. The fluidity of the battlefield inhibited B echelon personnel from replenishing their advanced troops.

(f) **Faulty concentration area/Too small a bridgehead/ Faulty tactics.** Pakistan crammed an armoured division and a substantial part of an infantry division into what appears to be an area less than 30-40 square kilometres and bounded by rivers, canals, and streams. In any event, creating a single small bridgehead for an entire armoured division to pass through would seem to work only if the lead armoured brigade attacks with utmost rapidity and violence. The lead brigade, 5 Armoured, would repeatedly get pushed back on the bridgehead, or would return on its own. Each time a brigade left the bridgehead, it was told to attack two or three divergent targets so that its effort was split. The shifting of units from one HQ to another or one sector to another, even as battles were underway was fateful.

(g) **Tank units too quick to recoil.** Because of a paucity of resources, both sides had little armour relative to the size of their armies. Because infantry was unable to protect itself against tanks even for a short time, tanks had to be dispersed in penny packets all over the battlefield for infantry support—even in armoured brigades and divisions. Tanks were valuable; they were also—in the absence of proper tank-infantry cooperation—highly vulnerable. The lack of reconnaissance information is remarkable: most of the time both sides were fighting almost blind over terrain with which they had little familiarity, and often with outdated, bad, or no maps at all. Given these circumstances, it is unsurprising that both sides tended to quickly recoil if they came upon each other unexpectedly. There was no conception of selecting an objective and sticking to it, taking the inevitable casualties as a necessary condition of success. Ironically, of course, the one time the Pakistanis did bash on regardless under pressure from the CGS and divisional commander, they drove into the Asal Uttar ambush. If the Pakistan armoured infantry had been properly trained, this would not have happened. Also, the integral reconnaissance troops of Pakistani armoured regiments were mounted on jeeps, so they could not operate boldly into the unknown.

(h) **Returning to leaguer at night.** Incredibly, after Pakistani tanks had pushed forward, often at cost, the moment darkness fell, the concern was solely to get back to a secure position. Thus, most of the gains of the day—sometimes all of the gains of the day—were surrendered.

(i) **Faulty Command and Control.** In the absence of a corps HQ, GOC 11 Division was given overall command of 1 Armoured Division as well. He had his hands full protecting his extended sector and maintaining his bridgehead, particularly with two of his seven manoeuvre units detached to the armoured brigade. This double-responsibility could not have helped a situation already bedevilled by bad leadership.

This did not end the battle of Khem Karan-Kasur. The Indians continued attacking until the ceasefire was announced. By 19 September, Pakistan had started to run of ammunition, aircraft spares, and reserve equipment. The Chief of the Army General Staff and the Chief of Air Staff met with the President of Pakistan that day to request a ceasefire be negotiated. Twenty-three days into the war, Pakistan was done for.

THE BATTLE OF BARKI

Introduction

Pakistan initiated the war in August 1965 with a misadventure in the Kashmir Sector. India retaliated in the plains and demonstrated its might in Punjab in the Ravi—Sutlej corridor.

11 Corps, deployed in Punjab, planned limited offensives along three axes to capture some territory and cause attrition an aim to secure territory up to the Eastern Bank of the Ichhogil Canal which was to be the forward line of penetration.

Plan

As a part of the 11 Corps offensive, 7 Infantry Division planned to attack in two phases:

a) **Phase 1.** Advance with 48 Infantry Brigade supported by a squadron of tanks less a troop (Central India Horse(CIH)) along axis Khalra-Barki, capture Barki and secure the bridge over the Ichhogil Canal by last light 6 September. Simultaneously an independent task force directly under 7 Infantry Division Headquarter comprising 17 Rajput and one tank troop (CIH), supported by a regiment of artillery and field company of engineers was to cross the border and secure Bedian by last light 6 September.

b) **Phase 2.** 65 Infantry Brigade to carry out mopping up operations along the canal and destroy all bridges within 7 Infantry Division area of responsibility.

48 Infantry Brigade and 65 Infantry Brigade concentrated close to the International Border astride the Khalra Barki axis. Preliminary operations commenced in the early hours of 6 September 1965. 4 Sikh (65 Infantry Brigade) and 6/8 Gorkha Rifles (48 Infantry Brigade) captured the assigned Pakistani Border Out Posts (BOPs) setting the stage for the advance by 48 Infantry Brigade to Ichhogil Canal, which commenced at 0500 hours on 6 September 1965. Initial progress was fairly rapid as no enemy opposition was encountered till the Hudiara Drain where a Pakistani company was holding a delaying position along the Drain. After a short but sharp engagement, Hudiara Drain was secured by 6/8 GR. 5 Guards, with a Squadron CIH under command, launched a day light attack on the Pakistani company holding defences in the area. The defenders, apprehending a threat to their flank and rear, chose to abandon Hudiara Drain after blowing up the bridge. 7 Infantry Division had achieved and exploited complete surprise to gain early advantage.

At this stage in order to retain the momentum, 48 Infantry Brigade was ordered to firm-in astride the axis along Hudiara Drain and engineers were ordered to construct a Bailey bridge over the Hudiara Drain which was accomplished with commendable speed by the afternoon of 7 September 1965. The bold moves kept the enemy guessing and offset his balance.

The Battle

With the change in plans, on the evening of 6 September, 65 Infantry Brigade was tasked to advance and capture the bridge over the Ichhogil Canal at Barki.

The strong point of Barki was well defended from all sides. The village was occupied by a Company of 17 Punjab (Pakistan) and 12 Punjab (Pakistan); many houses had been strengthened to be used as pill boxes and the narrow lanes made move of tanks impossible. To the defender, it offered good ambush sites and killing grounds, they had made tunnels and communication trenches to move undetected and safely between defended positions. Two companies occupied the West Bank of the Ichhogil Canal and prevented any outflanking move. The strong point was supported by elements of a Recce and Support Battalion and some tanks. A large number of fire units were placed under command and artillery support assured. Barki was indeed a fortress and, though a strong defensive position, it had to be secured before any assault on the Ichhogil Canal could be attempted.

65 Infantry Brigade supported by CIH less a squadron began its march from a firm base established by 16 PUNJAB at 0500 hours on 7 September with 9 MADRAS leading astride the axis Kalra-Barki. A number of preliminary operations were carried out to extend the firm base and break the outer crust of the defences for the final assault on Barki.

9 MADRAS captured Barka Kalan on the evening of 7 September and 4 SIKH captured Barka Khurd on 8 September.

4 SIKH was then tasked to capture Barki. The assault was supported by CIH less one squadron and 7 Artillery Brigade. After the capture of Barki, the battalion was to assist the crossing of the tanks over the Barki drain.

The attack began on the night of 10 September at 2000 hours from the East, which although a frontal approach was adopted because of domination of the other approaches from the defences on the canal. The enemy was well aware of the tactical importance of the strong point and fought back resolutely. Heavy artillery fire (over 2500 shells within 45 minutes) failed to deter the Sikhs who moved through the night like ghosts eliminating opposition in every street and house.

A well positioned Pakistani Machine gun was bringing down very effective fire on the attackers. Subedar Ajit Singh of a leading platoon was tasked to destroy the errant Machine gun. With utter disregard to personal safety, the valiant JCO charged the enemy position. A burst of machine gun fire wounded him in the chest but he carried on defiantly and went near enough to throw a grenade that effectively silenced the machine gun. His gallantry inspired his comrades and they routed the enemy but the Subedar succumbed to his injuries. For his bravery and supreme sacrifice, Subedar Ajit Singh was awarded the Maha Vir Chakra.

The assault was well supported by the tanks which fired and neutralised many pill boxes identified by the assaulting infantry. The tank fire was so accurate that the Pakistanis thought that Indians had bought new tanks with Night Firing capability. Other pillboxes were destroyed by lobbing grenades through their loop holes. Barki was finally captured after two hours of fierce hand to hand fighting.

Later when permission was given to the Pakistanis to collect their dead, they took away four truck loads including the body of Major Raja Aziz Bhatti who was posthumously awarded the Nishan-I¬Haider, Pakistan's highest gallantry award for his determined opposition to the 4 SIKH attack. Each year, Major Bhatti is honoured in Pakistan on 6 September, also known as Defence Day of Pakistan.

The brave Commanding Officer of CIH, Lt Col Satish Chandra Joshi won a Vir Chakra in the 1948 war against Pakistan. In the Battle for Barki he was driving a jeep to reconnoitre a passage through the mine field. However, a mine exploded killing the brave soldier who led from the front. He was awarded a bar to the Vir Chakra for his bravery and supreme sacrifice.

4 Sikh won one Maha Vir Chakra, three Vir Chakras, three Sena Medals, four Chief's Commendation Cards and the Battle Honour Barki for the daring assault on and capture of the heavily fortified Barki Strong Point.

While 4 SIKH were battling their way through Barki, 16 PUNJAB was moving towards Ichhogil Canal. The unit was tasked

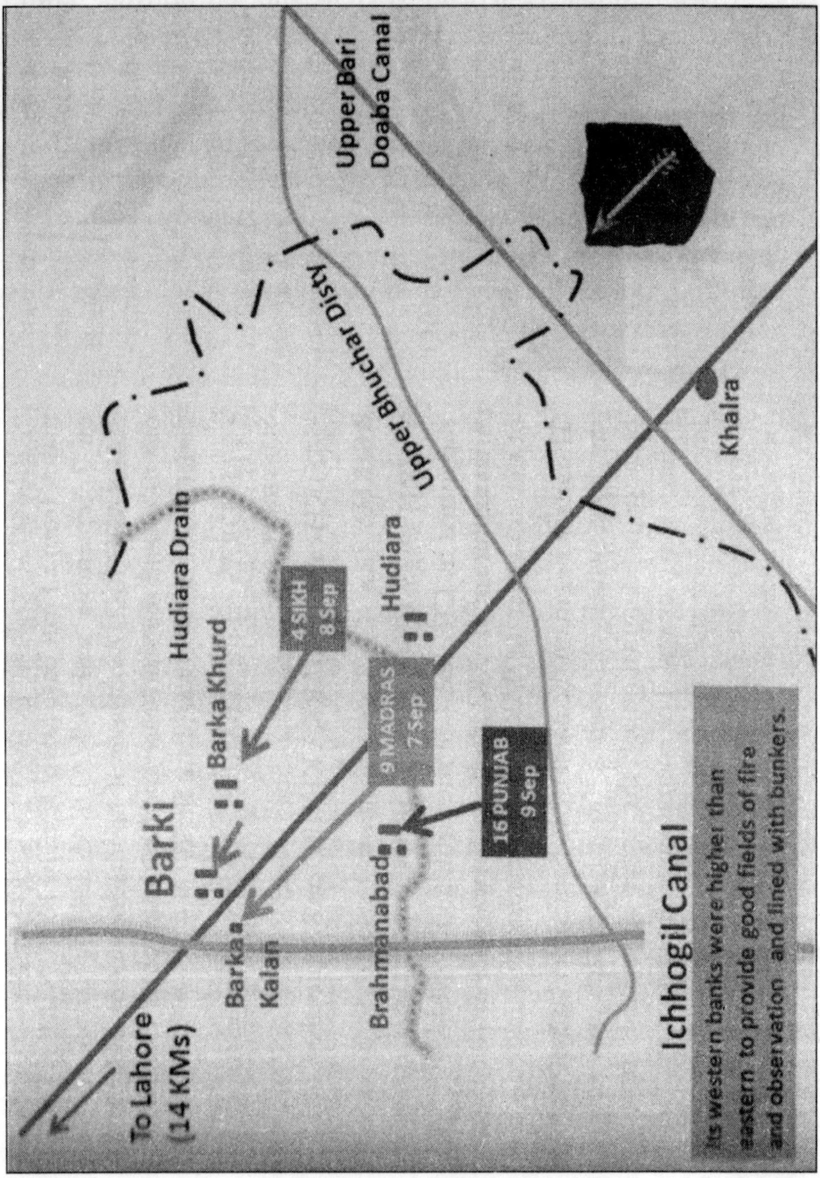

Map 11: Battle of Barki

to capture and demolish the bridge on Ichhogil canal near Barki village, 14 kilometres east of Lahore. The battalion rushed through the mine fields ahead of the canal to move forward to attack the enemy defences. The unit received one Vir Chakra, one Vishist Seva Medal, three Sena Medals and the Battle Honour of Barki. The Battalion had the distinction of operating its elements across the Ichhogil Canal. In the words of Lieutenant Colonel JS Bhullar, Commanding Officer of 16 PUNJAB:

> "So fierce was the assault that the enemy deserted their fire trenches and bunkers and tried to return by crossing the canal. In the melee and confusion of battle, they destroyed the bridge themselves. Many Pakistani soldiers were seen jumping into the canal. The battalion thus achieved the assigned task and objective."

Barki and the other captured areas in vicinity remained under the control of the Indian Army till the end of the war despite numerous attempts by Pakistan to dislodge them.

Analysis

7 Division was able to achieve surprise and make good progress. The enemy however quickly regrouped and fought back resolutely leading to a modification of the 7 Infantry Division plans. 65 Infantry Brigade responded with alacrity and did well to carry out preliminary attacks to expand their firm base and break the crust of the Barki strongpoint which was well defended, protected and organised for all round defence. All three battalions fought bravely and used their skills well to dislodge the well-entrenched and determined enemy. All objectives of 7 Infantry Division were achieved and the battalions honoured with the Battle Honour Barki.

The Ichhogil Canal and other drains and distributaries were well utilised by the defenders and protected Pakistan against any deep and destabilising thrust by the Indian Army. 16 PUNJAB had gained a foothold across Ichhogil and the capture of Barki provided a secure firm base for extending the bridgehead and launching an assault at Lahore. 7 Infantry Division operations could have been progressed further to threaten Lahore which was only 14 kilometres from Barki but that did not happen. The principle of reinforcement of success could have paid very rich tactical and strategically dividends; the Indian Army leadership however failed to exploit the gains.

> "*The Pakistani plan was based on BRB (Ichhogil Canal which to a great extent compensated for disparity in resources and enabled our formations in the Ravi-Sutlej Corridor to deploy on very extended frontages.*"
>
> ***—Commander-in-Chief Pakistan Army, General Muhammad Musa***

LIEUTENANT GENERAL HARBAKSH SINGH

INTRODUCTION

Lieutenant General Harbaksh Singh, Padma Vibhushan, Padma Bhushan, Vir Chakra, was one of the Indian Army's most reputed commanders. There are inspirational sagas attached to him in every battle that he fought till his retirement in 1969.

From 1948 Kashmir Operation to the 1965 war with Pakistan, Harbaksh Singh led his men from the front. Apart from the gallantry awards that he won, the general also had to his credit the incredible feat of having led on the battlefront a platoon, a company, a battalion, a brigade, a division, a corps and an army in his eventful career. A Japanese prisoner of war in the Second World War, stories of his exploits in Kashmir Operations, during 1947-48, have become legends.

In 1965, he commanded one of the biggest armies as the General Officer Commanding-in-Chief of Western Command against Pakistan. He was honoured with a Padma Bhushan for this splendid performance.

The words once used to describe Field Marshal Lord Wavell, seem apt for describing Lieutenant General Harbakhsh Singh: "He was essentially a soldier's soldier, and takes an assured place as one of the great commanders in military history".

EARLY LIFE

Born on 1 October 1913 in Badrukhan, in Sangrur, Harbaksh Singh was from a well-to-do peasant family. His father was a doctor who had joined the Jind State Forces and participated with the Jind Infantry in the Tirah Campaign of 1897-98, on the Northwest Frontier; in Mesopotamia during the First World War and in East Africa Later he was the Medical officer in-charge of the Military Hospital at Sangrur. His mother was a home-maker. Harbaksh Singh had three brothers and three sisters. He was the second of the four brothers.

He started his early education at Sangrur, at the age of three, when he started accompanying his elder brother to the local primary school. He completed his matriculation from the Ranbir High School at Sangrur.

His older brother, Gurbaksh Singh joined the First Battalion of the Jind Infantry as a Second Lieutenant. However, Harbaksh Singh went on to join the Government College at Lahore from where he studied for his B.A. He also became an accomplished hockey player. As he was keen on following a military career, he appeared in the Army Entrance Examination in June 1932 and was selected. He joined the Indian Military Academy (IMA) without appearing in the B/A. Examination as the call from the IMA came before the exam date.

Harbaksh Singh joined the India Military Academy in March 1933. He earned the spurs in equitation and was awarded the IMA Colours in swimming, hockey and athletics. He became an Under-officer of his company, leading it to win the Academy Colours as champion company. Perhaps he was the only Gentleman cadet who passed out of the IMA, after two and half year's stay without any punishment or blemish of any kind. He was commissioned in June 1935.

EARLY MILITARY CAREER

IC-31 Harbaksh Singh started his career with a year's post-commission attachment with the 2nd Battalion of the Argyl and Southerland Highlanders at Rawalpindi. Here he gained experience in fighting on the Northwest Frontier. After a year's attachment with the British battalion, he joined 5/11 Sikh Regiment at Aurangabad in July 1936.

In September 1938, the battalion moved to Razmak on the Northwest Frontier. Harbaksh Singh was initially the Signals Officer and then became a Company Commander. Here he honed his skills on Frontier warfare and its intricacies like organising of perimeter defences, organising of pickets for road protection and operations against the tribals.

In April 1939, the battalion moved to Malaya. Embarking from Madras, the battalion disembarked at Singapore and moved to Ipoh. The Second World War was imminent and the battalion got involved in training and preparing defences. Here he became the Adjutant of his battalion and remained so during the fighting against the Japanese on the Malay Peninsula. The battalion was initially deployed in the area of Kuanton and the Kuaton airfield when it got involved in the fighting against the Japanese. The operations became a series of withdrawal actions.

On 5 January 1942, Captain Harbaksh Singh was sent for by the Brigade Major and asked to reconnoitre the next defensive position for the Brigade. He took to the road on a motor-cycle, with his batman, Piara Singh, in the pillion seat, looking for a suitable place for defence along the road of withdrawal. After examining a position, which he did not like, he proceeded further along the road and fell prey to a Japanese ambush on the road. His head was hit by a splinter of a hand grenade or a mortar and he fell down, with the motorcycle and the pillion rider, and lost consciousness (this was recounted to him later in the prisoners-of-war camp by Piara Singh). He came to my senses only seventy-two hours later in Alexandra Hospital in Singapore. By then the surgeon had operated on his head, and put in a silver plate to cover the gash in his cranium. He was lucky to survive for the Japanese who had ambushed him had come down from the trees, from where they had lobbed the grenades, and had kicked both of them as they lay face down on the road and finding no response left them presuming they were dead. They were picked up later by a vehicle which was following and first taken to Battalion Headquarters, and then transferred to another vehicle and taken down the road to the road-head at Jeruntut. Before getting there, they had had to cross a ferry, which while being winched across was strafed by Japanese aircraft, and those who could run, left their vehicles, while Captain Harbaksh Singh lay there unconscious. Although some bullets hit his vehicle, he was unhurt. At Jeruntut railway station, he was attended to by a young captain, a surgeon, who dressed his wound and put him on the train, which also was bombed enroute by Japanese aircraft.

After a month's stay in Alexandra Hospital, he was evacuated to another hospital in Singapore. By then the mainland of Malaya had been evacuated by Allied troops. He was in a military hospital when General A.E Percival, the Allied field commander, surrendered all Allied forces in Malaya and Singapore to the Japanese in 1942.

On 10 February 1942, the Japanese entered Singapore and Captain Harbaksh Singh became a prisoner-of-war. His elder brother, Lieutenant Colonel Gurbaksh Singh, who was commanding the Jind Infantry was also a prisoner-of-war. The British and Indian prisoners-of-war were kept in separate camps. The latter were detained in the Bidadari Camp. Later they were shifted to the Kluang airfield. Then followed three years of miserable existence, and near-starvation, as a Japanese prisoner of war.

Life in the prisoner-of-war was tough. There was the added indoctrination by those who had defected to the Indian National Army. Lieutenant Colonel Gurbaksh Singh was the senior-most prisoner. Captain Harbaksh Singh managed to get hold of a wireless set from which they could news about the progress of the war. He also had opportunities to meet Netaji Subhas Chandra Bose and

General Mohan Singh of the Indian National Army but did not join their cause. He did, however, maintain cordial relations with them. The prolonged incarceration took its toll on the health of prisoners. It was a struggle to stay alive but religious fervour, humour, stealing rations and medicines; and growing vegetables kept them alive.

About his prisoner of war experience Lieutenant General Harbaksh Singh narrates that he had tried to follow certain principles in his life. He always believed in looking at the lighter side of life, whatever the circumstances. He followed this principle during his prisoner-of-war days, and because of it, he could claim to have come out of prison quite unaffected. In fact, when the Occupation Forces were being sent to Tokyo, he volunteered to go with them, but the medical authorities refused to accept his offer, for they felt that since he had been a prisoner-of-war, he undoubtedly nursed a grudge against the Japanese. He pleaded with them that this was not so, as, despite their notorious ill-treatment of prisoners-of-war, he held nothing against them. But they would just not believe him. He had learnt the lesson that if you are kind and considerate to your worst enemy, you can eventually win him over!

This had been brought home to him in a dramatic fashion, at the end of the War, when a British War-Crimes Investigation Team arrived at the prisoners-of-war camp. All the Japanese officers in station were lined up in front of them and they were asked to point out those officers who had been cruel to them. The camp commandant, Lieutenant Colonel Gurbakhsh Singh, who also happened to be his elder brother, had already warned them of their arrival and had instructed them not to lay blame on anyone. So, they remained silent. After the members of the team left, the senior-most Japanese officer, a Major General, drove up to their camp in his official car, with his flag flying and all that, and asked to speak to the commander of the camp. While they were wondering what calamity was to follow, Lieutenant Colonel Gurbakhsh Singh appeared in his usual torn and scanty attire, wooden clogs on his feet, and to their surprise, the Japanese Station Commander, resplendent in his uniform, bowed down low in front of his brother and with tears flowing down his cheeks, declared, in broken English: "You bigger man than myself'.

He then clicked his heels, turned around and walked past his car leaving it on the road in front of the camp commandant. After going about fifty yards, while they stood where they were absolutely stunned, he turned to his brother again, and bowing low asked for permission to take his cigarette-box out of the car. Lieutenant Colonel Gurbakhsh Singh nodded his assent, and the Japanese General clicking his heels once again, turned back, took his cigarette-box (a 555) out of the dash board of the car and walked away. The next day, the General sent his junior officer and handed over a complete list of vehicles, arms and stores in their possession, as they were now their prisoners-of-war!

Lieutenant General Harbaksh Singh also believed that to a large extent one controls one's own destiny. Released at the end of the war in 1945, he remained in hospital, at Ambala, for some months with beri-beri and other problems brought on by malnutrition and inhuman conditions in Japanese POW camps.

I April 1945, he was posted as second-in-command of 4 Sikh at Campbellpur, on release from hospital. He was perhaps the only deputy ever to ride a horse on parade in an infantry battalion, as he was too weak to march.

In 1947 he completed the Long Staff Course at Quetta and was posted as GSO-1 (Operations and Training), Eastern Command. However, he was ill with flu and fever and admitted to the hospital at Ambala on reaching back to India from Quetta. It was on 29 October 1947, while in hospital that he heard of the death of Lieutenant Colonel Dewan Ranjit Rai, of 1 Sikh, to enemy bullets near Baramulla in Kashmir.

Lieutenant Colonel Harbaksh Singh volunteered to command the battalion. But he was posted as deputy commander at the headquarters of 161 Infantry Brigade.

KASHMIR OPERATIONS: 1947-48

India became independent on 15 August 1947, and Pakistani-backed regulars, irregulars and tribesmen crossed into the state of Jammu and Kashmir on 22 October. In spite of a determined effort by the J&K state forces and by the initially inducted Indian troops, the enemy reached the outskirts of Srinagar, within a week, and the fall of the capital city was imminent.

On the directions of the Deputy Military Secretary at Army Headquarters, Lieutenant Colonel Harbaksh Singh reported for duty to the HQ Delhi and East Punjab Command for further instructions. The GOC-in-C, Lieutenant General Russel, said that he should get ready to leave for Srinagar by air first thing the next morning, not as Commanding Officer of 1 Sikh, but as Deputy Brigade Commander to 161 Infantry Brigade, being inducted at the time in the Valley.

On 1 November 1947, Lieutenant Colonel Harbaksh Singh left for Srinagar in the first civilian aircraft to leave Safdarjung Aerodrome that morning. As the aircraft neared the airfield at Srinagar, a pall of smoke could be seen over every village around the plateau of the landing-strip, an unmistakable sign of arson and destruction by the Pakistani Raiders.

The first Indian Army officer to meet him at the airfield was Lieutenant Colonel Pritam Singh. He described the military situation and handed over the situation saying that a battle was raging at the time on the perimeter of the airfield, where about 200 Raiders, having burnt and looted the village of Ilgam, were engaging a platoon strength of his battalion, a mere 30 riflemen. He had, at that time, only one Company defending the entire airfield.

While being briefed, Lieutenant Colonel Harbaksh Singh noticed parts of a mountain gun being off-loaded by some Sikh troops from one of the aircrafts that had landed after his. He walked up to the young Sikh officer, supervising the unloading of the equipment, and recognised him as Second Lieutenant Jabar Jang Singh of Patiala State Forces, his own nephew. He informed him that his instructions were to deliver these two mountain guns, which were the property of the Indian Army, and had been on loan to the Patiala State Forces for the duration of the Second World War, to the airfield and return with his crew to Patiala. He had strict orders not to participate in the fighting in Kashmir, as Patiala State had not yet decided to merge with India and did not, in any way, wish to interfere with the 'internal affairs' of a sister state—Kashmir.

Lieutenant Colonel Harbaksh Singh told him of the fighting near the airfield and, using his influence as his uncle, asked him to order his crew to assemble the guns and pull them behind the only jeep theer, to the perimeter of the airfield, where a mere infantry platoon was gallantly facing a much larger force of Raiders. Jabar Jang Singh pulled out of his pocket a written order, signed by the Commander-in-Chief of the Patiala State Forces, the Maharaja himself, which clearly stated that these men of his were, under no circumstances, to take part in the fighting in Srinagar. Lieutenant Colonel Harbaksh Singh read the order, folded the paper carefully and put it in his pocket. He then drew his attention to the critical situation near the airfield and hinted that if the Raiders were to gain a foothold on the perimeter of the airfield his departure to Patiala by air would be in jeopardy. Second Lieutenant Jabar Jang Singh decided to consult his men. Lieutenant Colonel Harbaksh Singh, watching them from where he stood, realised that they did not seem to be interested in embroiling themselves in the fighting.

Walking up to them stiffly and calling them to attention, he shouted: "As Senior Commander in the field area I order you to assemble your guns and follow me". As for the written order from their Commander-in-Chief, he drew their attention to the well-known Field Service Regulation which enjoins that an order given by a Superior Commander can be disobeyed, or altered, by a Field Commander on the spot, provided the latter was fully satisfied that this needed to be done, and could justify it later. Pointing his finger at the young officer, he said: "Should you disobey my order, I will have you summarily court-martialled and shot for showing cowardice in front of the enemy, under the powers I enjoy as a Force

Commander in Battle". The havildar with the gun detachment, thereupon, quickly responded that his men were ready to carry out the orders, but, unfortunately, the guns they had brought from Patiala were without their sights and could thus not be used. Lieutenant Colonel Harbaksh Singh explained that this did not present a problem, as the distance to be covered to hit the target, where the Raiders were assembled at the edge of the airfield, was so short that they would be required to only fire 'direct', through open sights! The detachment had no choice but to obey orders, and once they saw the jumbled enemy and the havoc their shots were causing among the fleeing Raiders, it was difficult to stop them from firing. The gamble of Lieutenant Colonel Harbaksh Singh had worked. The Raiders, who had had every intention of attacking the airfield, dispersed helter-skelter with the appearance of artillery realising that their objective was now out of reach. No serious attempt was made by them, thereafter, to threaten the airfield and the much needed reinforcements of manpower and equipment continued to arrive by air undisturbed.

Battle of Shalateng

1 Sikh, after its gallant action at Baramulla had withdrawn to Pattan which was considered too far away from Srinagar for the effective defence of Srinagar, which required more compact defences. 1 Sikh was, consequently, ordered to withdraw to Shalateng, just outside Srinagar, on 4 November. If the back of the enemy could be broken here, an offensive could then be undertaken to drive the invaders out of the valley. Accordingly, 1 Sikh took up positions along a spill channel and bund.

On 7 November, information was received that a large force of around 3,000 of the enemy had concentrated in area Milestone 4 (6 kilometres) preparing to attack the Srinagar. Subsequently, there was intense fire by the raiders. 161 Infantry Brigade planned to attack the enemy with 1 Kumaon supported by armoured cars of 7 Cavalry. Colonel Harbakhsh Singh, then second-in-command of the newly inducted 161 Brigade, was given the task of conducting the battle.

Accordingly, the 7 Cavalry squadron was ordered to move to the vicinity of the enemy and open fire on them from the rear. While this was done, 1 Kumaon assaulted them from a flank. In a brilliantly planned and executed operation, the enemy was completely taken by surprise and ran helter-skelter leaving 472 enemy dead on the field. The Air Force also inflicted heavy casualties on the fleeing raiders. Having suffered heavy casualties, the enemy never recovered thereafter and began to retreat. The threat to Srinagar was now over. If the capital city had fallen, it would have been one of the greatest disasters in Indian history.

The Battle of Shalateng thus paved the way of the eviction of the enemy and making the Valley safe. Indeed, it was a decisive victory. The battles around Srinagar, although small in terms of size of forces involved were the most crucial battles of the Kashmir War.

Command of 1 Sikh

On 12 December 1947, on hearing about the heavy casualties suffered by 1 Sikh, Colonel Harbakhsh Singh, proceeded to Uri and took over the command of the battalion voluntarily, shedding a star from his rank. He brought back the battalion to Srinagar and rehabilitated it. However, even before the rehabilitation was complete, the battalion was called out to fight the enemy who had crossed the snow-clad Pharikian ki Gali and had occupied Handwara. In a rare display of military leadership, he led the truncated battalion, in one of the most daring operations in Indian military history.

On 7 February 1948, it was learnt that the raiders, in thousands, had captured the State Forces post at Trahagam. Thus, the whole Trahagam Valley fell into their hands and they were moving to capture Handwara-Sopore and then advance on towards Srinagar. 1 Sikh, which was then at Srinagar (after having been pulled back from Uri) with a troop of armoured cars of 7 Cavalry were tasked to deal with the threat. By the time the battalion reached the area, it was learnt that the raiders, under the command of Pakistan army regulars, had occupied Handwara.

The swift reaction by 1 Sikh caused the raiders to pull back. The battalion continued in pursuit of the fleeing enemy and Kupwara was reached by nightfall of 11 February. Trahagam was reoccupied the next day.

The advent of summer in 1948 brought about in its wake, the right climate for the conduct of offensive operations in the Kashmir Valley. After the threat to Srinagar was removed and Indian forces consolidated themselves in the Uri area, the spring of 1948 was utilised for reorganisation of the command structure and for preparations for launching a major offensive, with a view to rid the Kashmir Valley of the aggressors. By the middle of May 1948, the forces were ready for launching the projected offensive.

Operations of 163 Infantry Brigade

Promoted to command 163 Brigade, Brigadier Harbakhsh Singh led one of the two brigades launched by General Thimmaya, then in command of Sri Division (later 19 Infantry Division) to clear the enemy out of the Jhelum valley, up to Muzaffarabad and Domel. In a conference of formation commanders on 13 May 1948, General Thimayya gave out his appreciation. The advance was likely to be contested; therefore surprise and speed were important. A series of night attacks were to be launched to ensure success. Briefly, the main thrust was to be along the Uri–Domel road by 161 Infantry Brigade, which was to be relieved by a newly inducted Brigade (77 Para Brigade). 163 Infantry Brigade was to carry out a diversionary operation towards Tithwal from Handwara two or three days earlier, in order to draw as much of the enemy reserve as possible from Muzaffarabad. 163 Brigade had to move over the Nasta Chun Pass to Tithwal and beyond.

In the Handwara Sector, the ground rose up to the Nastachun Pass and then descended into the Tithwal Valley. This valley was flanked by high mountains on either side; and their capture was essential before Tithwal could be secured. After Tithwal, the Kishenganga River had to be crossed, before further moves could be undertaken to Muzaffarabad. Brigadier Harbaksh Singh planned to advance to the Nastachun Pass along two axes, namely, Handwara–Dogarpur–Nastachun with Brigade less a battalion and Handwara–Kupwara–Trahagam–Chokibal–Nastachun with a Battalion group. After securing Nastachun, the advance was to continue to Tithwal, along the hills on either side of the valley.

163 Infantry Brigade (1 Madras, 1 Sikh, 3 Garhwal) commenced its operations on 18 May, as planned. Dogarpur and Trahagam were captured by 1 Madras and 3 Garhwal respectively on 19 May. Since the resistance on the 3 Garhwal front appeared to be more intense, 1 Sikh was sent on an outflanking move to capture Chowkibal, which they did on 20 May. Subsequently, 1 Madras captured the Nastachun Pass on 21 May. This vital pass was thus secured in good time and the enemy's plans were completely disrupted. The enemy suffered considerable casualties and his morale was shaken. This operation had opened the way for the capture of Tithwal.

The advance to Tithwal was continued on 22 May, with 1 Sikh leading and on the next day it was captured by the Brigade; and the hills on either side of the Valley cleared. Thereafter, a battalion was put across the Kishanganga and it captured the high ground on the opposite side. However, under intense pressure of counter-attacks from the enemy and owing to difficulties of support across the river, the battalion had to be called back. In the Tithwal area, 6 Rajputana Rifles cleared an important hill feature, during which Sepoy Piru Singh displayed gallantry of a high order and was awarded the Param Vir Chakra, posthumously. In the same sector, repeated counter-attacks by the enemy were repulsed in Richhmar Gali by 1 Sikh and L/Nk Karam Singh was awarded the Param Vir Chakra for displaying valour of a high order.

In six days, Brigadier Harbakhsh Singh had in a lightning move secured all territory starting from Handwara to the Kishanganga over the Nasta Chun Pass and Tithwal after fighting aggressive battles.

General Thimayya instructed Brigadier Harbaksh Singh, Commander 163 Infantry Brigade, to plan Operation 'Suriya' for the thrust from Tithwal towards Muzaffarabad. The task of the brigade was to capture the high ground west of Muzaffarbad and Domel. The operation could not be carried out due to inadequacy of forces with 163 Infantry Brigade. 1 Madras and 1 Sikh were occupying posts, only 3 Garhwal Rifles was available. As two battalions, at least, were required for the operation, 2/4 Gorkha Rifles, then at Chowkibal, was allotted to the brigade. However, the supply situation was extremely bleak as there were barely a day's rations available with the brigade, which needed seven days of stocks to launch the operation. Stocking was only possible with mules and porters and the weather did not permit air maintenance. The brigade was, therefore, ordered to consolidate its positions at Tithwal and maintain contact with the enemy through rigorous patrolling.

As part of the defence of Tithwal, the ridge across the Kishanganga River was occupied and picquets established. An attempt was also made to secure Richmar Gali and the Mir Kalsi ridge, to serve as a springboard for the advance towards Muzaffarabad. The occupation of these features by 1 Sikh resulted in fierce enemy efforts to recapture them. There was heavy fighting on 2 and 3 June, which resulted in beating back the enemy. However, the enemy build-up continued and the whole sector came under regular and sustained artillery and mortar shelling.

The enemy attacked the 163 Infantry Brigade forward positions across the Kishanganga River on 8 July. The picquets had to be evacuated the next day. In what was a serious setback, the Mir Kalsi ridge positions were also withdrawn. 6 Rajputana Rifles was then allotted to 163 Infantry Brigade for an offensive, on 15 July, to sweep the enemy away from the ridge which stretched towards Raniwala Dana. 1 Sikh also successfully defended their position at Richmar Gali against a determined enemy attack on 20 July.

Citation for Vir Chakra

In May 1948, Brigadier Harbaksh Singh, Commander 163 Brigade, was ordered to advance and capture Tithwal with a view to capturing the enemy's base from where he operated towards the Handwara valley and to cut his advance from Muzzaffarabad to Gurais. The tribesmen were then adopting guerilla warfare to infiltrate the Kashmir Valley.

On the night of 16 May, Brigadier Harbaksh Singh, leading his troops on foot, made a rapid advance through a very difficult terrain, including the crossing of the 11,000-ft. Nastachun Pass, and completely surprised the enemy who broke and withdrew in confusion and panic in all directions. Tithwal was thus captured on 23 May. The success of the operations was to a very great extent due to his personal leadership.

During the subsequent consolidation at Tithwal, when the enemy concentrated a stronger force and brought heavy fire to bear with numerous counter-attacks, Brigadier Harbaksh Singh visited every position placing troops on the ground and was frequently under enemy fire. To keep himself in touch with Divisional HQ he made frequent trips on foot unmindful of the danger of being ambushed as the line of communication was still exposed to enemy infiltration.

During these operations, Brigadier Harbaksh Singh showed gallantry and courage of a very high order and his personal appearance in forward posts, without regard for personal safety, considerably cheered the defenders.

SUBSEQUENT MILITARY CAREER

After the Kashmir operations, he went on to serve as the deputy commandant of the Indian Military Academy dropping his rank to Colonel. Later he was BGS at the Western Command headquarters; Director of Infantry at the Army headquarters, and in 1957 attended a course at the Imperial Defence College, UK. In January 1959, he became the first foreign officer to go on attachment with German Army's first division to be raised after its devastation in World War II.

He returned to India to take over as the General Officer Commanding of 27 Infantry Division, and later as the GOC of 5 Infantry Division. From July 1961 to October 1962, he was the Chief of Staff at the Western Command headquarters.

When the Chinese invaded NEFA and Ladakh, he was moved from Shimla to take over the command of 4 Corps headquarters. And later he moved as the GOC of 33 Corps.

After his posting with the 33 Corps, he was appointed as the GOC-in-C of the Western Command, whose area used to stretch from down south to Kashmir. He led the Western Command successfully against the Pakistan Army along the entire border. The outstanding leadership of Lieutenant General Harbaksh Singh had played a key role in boosting the morale of a defeated army turning it into a striking force within just three years of the Chinese encounter.

The general was honoured with a Padma Vibhusan, a rare honour for a military man.

He retired in September 1969.

1965 WAR WITH PAKISTAN

War clouds gathered once again in 1965. Pakistan took the offensive in April in Kutch and was successfully repulsed. In August, Kashmir became the target and on 6 September India went to war.

In the war of 1965 the decision taken was to move units from their peacetime locations directly into battle and to cross the international border simultaneously at a fixed time to achieve total surprise. This retaliatory attack across the border in Punjab was necessitated by Pakistan's unprovoked attack in the Chhamb sector. The Indian strategy worked.

Pakistan was unprepared for the massive assault at 4 a.m. on 6 September 1965 by forces which seemed to have materialised overnight, and which now posed a threat to Lahore. As for preparing the troops "mentally", extensive war games had already taken place two months earlier and troops were mentally prepared to go into battle in the event of war.

The western Army offensive across the Punjab border which started at 4.30 a.m. on 6 September went well and 3 Jat, under a very able commander, Lieutenant Colonel Desmond Hayde, crossed the Ichhogil Canal and reached the Bata factory on the outskirts of Lahore. However, the commander of the 54 Infantry Brigade asked him to withdraw on 6 September itself, to a point not even on the Ichhogil Canal but 2,000 yards short of it on the Indian side.

The situation on the ground saw a turn when Pakistan counter attacked 4Mountain Division on the 11 Corps left flank at Khemkaran. 4 Mountain Division comprising 62 and 7 Brigades, a strength of six infantry battalions, lost two-and-a-half battalions in a matter of hours, less through enemy action and more by desertion, and was virtually overrun.

The situation on 7 September afternoon was grim, while 4 Mountain Division fell back to the village of Asal Uttar and hurriedly prepared a defended sector based on the surviving three-and-a-half battalions and the 2 (Independent) Armoured Brigade. On 9 September, Pakistan's 1 Armoured Division, whose location till then was not known, attacked 4 Mountain Division. In the ensuing battle, their operational order was captured. The plan was to attack and overrun the weak 4 Mountain Division while a strong combat group was to cut the lines of communication of both 4 Mountain Division and 7 Infantry Division on the Barki Axis and finally to cut the GT Road at the Beas Bridge, effectively sealing off 11 Corps HQs and Corps troops at Raya, and the line of communication of 15 Infantry Division in one sweep. The situation was extremely grim and some panic set in.

Having returned to HQ Western Army at Ambala, from 4 Mountain Division, at midnight on the 9 September and after a visit to the operations room, the Army Commander retired for three hours rest before leaving at four' clock the next morning. The instructions to his ADC, was not to awaken him unless it was urgent. At 2.30 a.m. the Army Chief, General J.N. Chaudhary, called and spoke to the General and after a heated discussion centred around the major threat that had developed, the Chief asked the Army Commander to consider withdrawal of 11 Corps to hold a line on the Beas river. Lieutenant General Harbakhsh Singh refused to carry out this order.

The next morning, 4 Mountain Division stabilised the position and when the Chief visited command headquarters at Ambala that afternoon, 10 September, the crisis was over and the subject was not discussed. Had Lieutenant General Harbakhsh Singh acquiesced and ordered a withdrawal, not only would have half of Punjab been under Pakistani occupation but the morale of the Indian Army would have been rock bottom, affecting operations in other theatres as well.

The decision to send 4 Sikh to invest Khem Karan was taken with the aim of hitting the enemy already reeling from a major reverse, having lost 99 tanks (captured or destroyed) during the previous two days. It was a tactically sound decision aimed at taking advantage of that fleeting opportunity to strike the enemy when he was off-balance. That it did not work is no reflection on the soundness of the decision.

ASSESSMENT AS A MILITARY COMMANDER

Lieutenant General Harbakhsh Singh was indeed a remarkable man of whom every Indian should be proud. He was a man of many talents, a sportsman, an athlete, accomplished horse rider but, above all, a soldier's soldier for his many considerations to his subordinates and Jawans alike. These are mentioned repeatedly in his book. During the Second World War he was taken prisoner by the Japanese. He and his brother, an officer in the Jind State Army, refused overtures from General Mohan Singh, and later from Netaji Subash Chandar Bose himself to join the Indian National Army. Back in India during the Jammu and Kashmir operations he won decisive battles at Shelatang and Tithwal and his Brigade was poised to attack Muzaffarabad in Operation Surya when he was transferred. "Operation Surya" never took place.

The Indians conceived a fine plan to outflank Muzaffarabad and executed a brilliant brigade level march across against the 3,000 metres plus high Nastachun Pass, thus unexpectedly forcing their way with great ease to Tithwal. The Pakistani official history noted

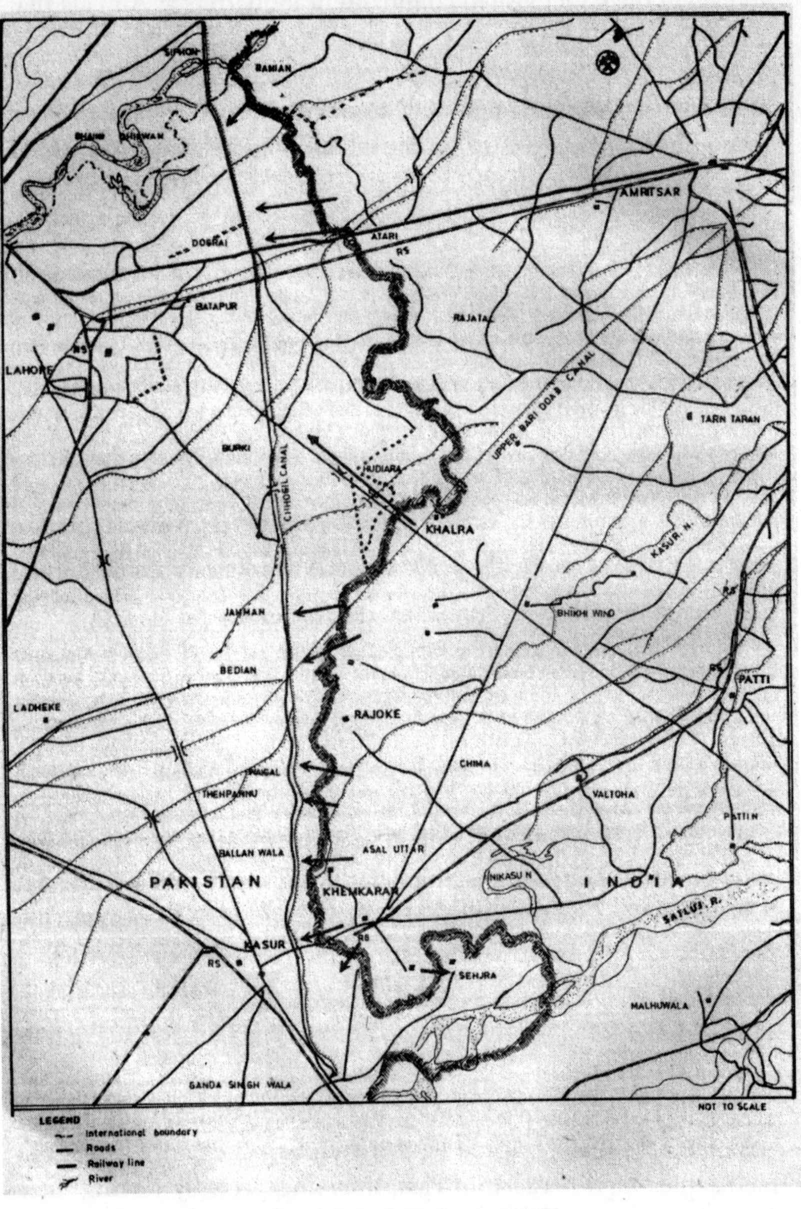

Map 12: Lahore Sector, 1965

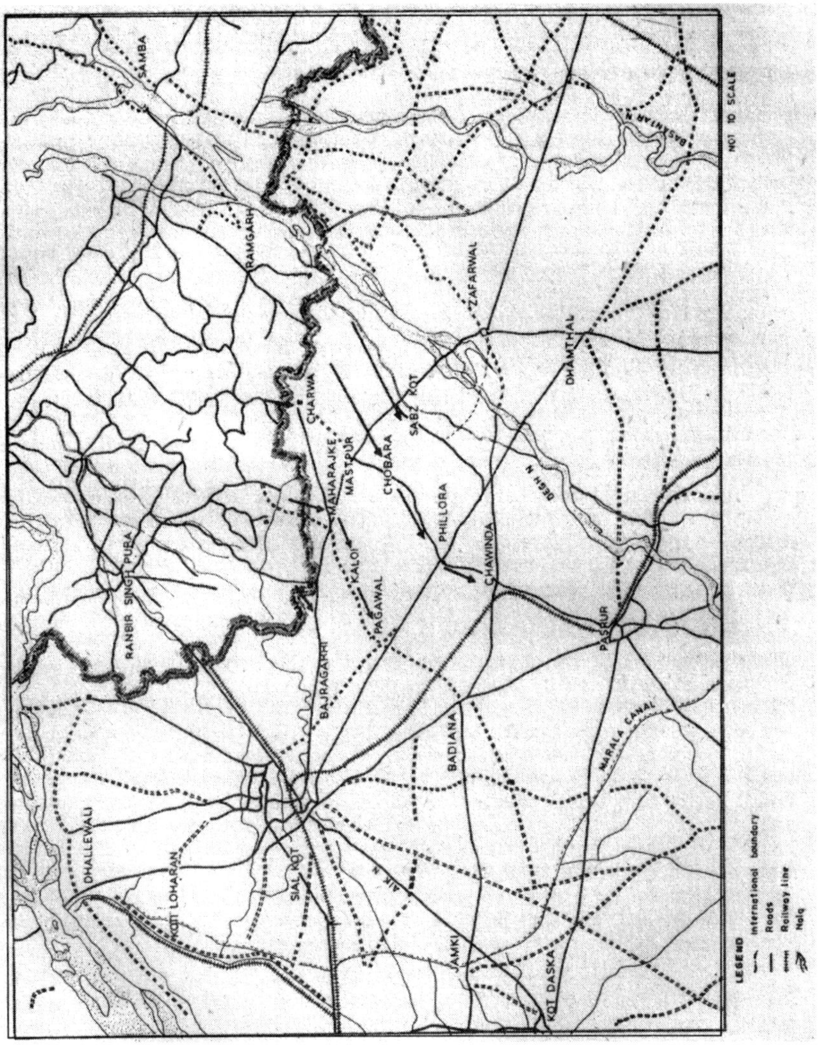

Map 13: Sialkot Sector, 1965

"Brigadier Harbaksh Singh, commander of the 163 Brigade waited at Tithwal for two days to let the rest of his brigade join him there. He lingered a little longer to prepare for his next move and perhaps also to coordinate his moves with that of the Indian offensive in the Jhelum Valley for a two pronged push towards Muzaffarabad. This delay changed the subsequent course of history in Kishanganga Valley, as it enabled the first two companies of 4/16 Punjab under Major Mohammad Akbar Khan to reach by a forced march in the vicinity of Tithwal and take up positions there". The Pakistanis saved their position by reinforcing it with a brigade.

Lieutenant General Harbakhsh Singh's greatest challenge came during the Indo-Pakistan War of 1965 when he was Western Army Commander based at Simla. Enemy attack across the international border in Punjab did not materialise as he had expected due to failures by others at several fronts. Yet he remained fearless and undaunted. At one time there was panic at Army Headquarters that Pakistan might break through Indian defences. Lieutenant Harbakhsh Singh's finest moment came when the Army Chief, General Chaudhry, ordered him "to abandon Amritsar and set-up a defence line behind the river Beas." Rightly, Lieutenant General Harbakhsh Singh refused such an order, and the threat to Amritsar never developed. Although Pakistan was contained and battered at many places but it was not decisively beaten. Lieutenant General Harbakhsh Singh nowhere mentions in his book that India won the 1965 War.

Lieutenant General Harbaksh Singh's book, 'Line of Duty', begins with setting the motto, the goals and a set of ethics and the ethos by which he charted his personal compass. Interspersed between the accounts of battles are anecdotal encounters that turned defeat into victory.

Lieutenant General Harbakhsh Singh was sharply critical of higher commanders in Kashmir like General Kulwant Singh and Brigadier L.P. Sen whom he called 'Bogey the Bogus" for failing to chase out the raiders, blocking their re-entry and ending altogether the cancerous Kashmir problem. Sen dubbed Singh "Hairbrush" and was in turn called "Son of a Gun" in verse.

There are many fresh insights on the 1965 war. For example, Harbaksh wrote about Sikh gunners abandoning their guns and fleeing Akhnur, cases of widespread desertion of members of the infantry (surprisingly, the Gurkhas) from the Ichhogil front, 4 Sikh walking into a Pakistani trap in Khemkaran and several instances of un-commander like behaviour of senior officers. Of course, Lieutenant General Harbakhsh Singh did not mention, though it was well known in military circles, that he goaded 4 Sikh to undertake an impossible mission to commemorate their Regimental Day.

A possible reason why the war did not go well in Western Command in 1965 may have been that Lieutenant General Harbakhsh Singh had difficulty in getting along with the then Army Chief General J.N. Chaudhuri. There are conflicting accounts of who gave the orders to abandon the Amritsar salient to fall back on the River Beas which luckily, did not happen.

The Pakistani offensive plan i.e. a thrust against Indian line of communication at Akhnur in case of a limited war in Kashmir or/ and against Indian line of communication between Indian Corps holding Ravi-Sutlej Corridor at Jandiala Guru on Amritsar-Jullundhur road in case of an all out war was brilliant in conception. This was so because if successful any of the two plans would have forced the Indians to sue for peace at best and to surrender at worst. Lieutenant General Harbakhsh Singh averred:

> "A Blitzkrieg deep into our territory towards the Grand Trunk Road or the Beas Bridge would have found us in the helpless position of a commander paralysed into inaction for want of readily available reserves while the enemy was inexorably pushing deep into our vitals. It is a nightmarish feeling even when considered in retrospect at this stage".

THE VICTORIOUS WILL

In the experience of Lieutenant General Harbakhsh Singh, he who plays 'safe' lies low and awaits developments, usually comes off second best. The Commander who always tries to dominate a situation, is eager to seize the fleeting opportunities of war and is prepared to pounce upon the enemy with inspired 'audacity, usually carries the day, however adverse the circumstances of the battle. There are always more ways than one of fighting a battle successfully, but few of winning it cheaply. For while the rigid, slow plodder, the stickler for text book conventions, too, reaches the goal, his route of success is often littered with prohibitive costs in men and material. Quick, spectacular achievements, at comparatively low cost usually come to the audacious, the bold and the enterprising in battle.

The Cult of the Victorious Will

Military history is replete with examples of missed opportunities leading to disastrous setbacks in battle.

During the 1965 War with Pakistan, there were a series of brilliant offensive actions but interspersed, far too frequently, with instances where we failed to take advantage of favourable situations through lack of enterprise. Often, we found the enemy reeling, but the knockout blow came too late, or not at all. The uncanny instinct with which successful commanders spotted the passing chance in battle, and the alacrity with which they exploited these fleeting opportunities, makes inspiring reading. The instinct of the opportunity in action is often inborn—but it can also be cultivated through training and psychological development. It is a sad commentary on our training techniques, both during tactical exercise without troops and exercises with troops that the rigid application of accepted tactical doctrines is often unimaginatively insisted upon—the unconventional is often frowned upon, whatever the justification of such action. The inevitable—'well, it is not usually done'—dampens the spirit of the average officer during training, thus curbing his initiative in war.

While I am all for teaching correct procedures, drills and precepts of war, it must be appreciated that these are all means to an end—

not the end in themselves; and once mastered, the average officer must retain an elasticity of mind to vary, deviate or depart from them to take advantage of a favourable situation. To do this, he must be encouraged to develop a mental attitude which, while respecting the established conventions of war, is, nevertheless, prepared to break away from them should the occasion so demand. There is therefore a definite requirement for a re-orientation in our attitude and methods of training. We should aim at cultivating in our Commanders a spirit and mental attitude which would welcome chances of bold action instead of indecisive wavering when faced with a situation.

Reorientation of Training Techniques

I give in the succeeding paragraphs a few general ideas and guidance for imparting the type of training I have in mind. I expect you to study them with care and implement them with imagination.

While in the initial stages, the correct application of established principles should be taught and practised once a sound foundation in this respect is laid, variations from accepted norms should be permitted and even encouraged, within reason. In exercises, situations should be created involving:

- the taking of calculated risks;
- the use of bold and audacious action, even at the risk of deviating from normal procedures and established principles of warfare.

The average officer should be impressed with the conviction that if a gamble is justified he must not hesitate to stake his all. The ideal, of course, would be achieved when an officer is so psychologically attuned to the offensive spirit that not only is he on the lookout for the opportune moment in battle, but also eager to create for himself a favourable situation for bold action.

I have often noticed during tactical exercises, without troops/ sand-model exercises, that even at lower levels most of the time is devoted to stereotyped and hypothetical problems, repeated with monotonous regularity; the 'action' required being pushed to the background and sometimes even ignored. It must be remembered that in battle it is more often the cumulative effect of a series of 'conduct actions' that carries the day and not the best laid plans on papers. While saying this, I do not deprecate the importance of planning but am against the disproportionate time devoted to what I call 'passive' training as opposed to 'active' problems associated with the conduct of the various individuals concerned on the battlefield. Problems requiring quick decision and involving aggressive action should be liberally introduced in tactical exercises without troops and in exercises with troops. It is more a question of laying the appropriate emphasis on a particular aspect of training.

Problems requiring syndicate solutions should be "reduced to the minimum and generally interspersed with individual requirements. For, while 'committee' planning is inevitable on account of the complexity of modern warfare, the ability to make individual, on the spot, decisions is vital in the battlefield. An officer loses his capacity for independent thought and action if he is 'habituated' exclusively to syndicate work.

Nothing is more demoralising in war than inaction. The hesitant, the wary and cautious usually induce despair and despondency in their subordinates. This tendency must be ruthlessly stamped out during training. It must be impressed on all that any action, especially when the circumstances are grim and the situation confused, is better than listless waiting and hoping for the best. The type who is inclined to look over his shoulder for orders or requires prodding from the rear, must either change his attitude or quit a command appointment.

In exercises, some Commanders tend to take for granted the smooth functioning of supply lines, reliable communications, fault-less transmission of orders and flawless execution of plans, not realising that in war the malfunctioning of these agencies is the rule rather than the exception. During training, problems should be posed to depict the unexpected in war so that Commanders are mentally conditioned to take such situations in their stride rather than being paralysed into inaction. No 'imponderable' in war should be allowed to interfere with the tempo of action in battle.

The fog of war should be treated as a normal phenomenon in battle. The practice to base plans and actions on detailed information about the enemy glibly supplied by obliging umpires during exercises must be discouraged, as such an unrealistic training will habituate the average officer into expecting similar detailed information about the enemy during battle also. It is admitted that intelligence about the enemy is important but waiting for its complete fulfilment is fatal, especially where time favours the opponent. One must be trained to accept that in war more often than not, only scanty information about the enemy will be available and the gaps in the jigsaw puzzle will have to be filled-in by intelligent deduction, and even through sheer guesswork. The tendency to hold back action because adequate information is not readily forthcoming is the favourite refuge of the type who likes to play 'safe' - and 'safety' in the battlefield is synonymous with cowardice.

Conclusion

There comes a time in most battles when the opposing sides are evenly matched and vital issues hang in the balance. It is at this juncture, when the original plans and orders have gone hay-wire, that the Commander with greater stamina, grit and determination will rally his troops for one final, desperate effort and tip the scales in his favour. The will to outlast the opponent, the ability to draw on one last ounce of strength for this final, audacious fling at the enemy is the hallmark of a great field Commander. This must be emphasised in all training. For remember, as Napoleon said 'the fate of the battle is the result of a moment, of a thought! A mental flash decides and the last reserve accomplishes the object.'

It is a mistaken concept that the cult-of the 'victorious will' finds expression only amongst Commanders engaged in offensive operations. This is not so. Even in defence, when there is a danger of armour overrunning a locality, it is troops infused with audacity who will fire their anti-tank weapons to the last and then 'ducking down' let the enemy tanks pass overhead, but only to emerge again from their trenches to take the tanks from the rear. Bold and daring tank-hunting parties led by inspired Non-Commissioned Officers can play havoc with any intruding armour which may have escaped the fire of anti-tank weapons in the defensive localities.

The need for injecting a bold, daring and audacious attitude in our Commanders is vitally necessary, for in war the timing of an action and the speed of its mounting is all important. We must prefer the officer who acts and makes mistakes to the one who is never wrong, by playing 'safe'. I would, however, like to sound a word of warning here. A misplaced interpretation of the ideas I have given above may, if applied unimaginatively, produce the type who breaks conventions merely because he thinks it is fashionable to do so or who, under the mistaken guise of audacity, tries to play rashly with the lives of men. This must be guarded against. The aim of training I have in mind is to forge a Commander who blends a cool and calm mind with the swift and sure intuition of spotting and grasping the transitory chances in war and then acting on them with paralysing speed, delivers to the enemy the 'coupe de grace'. These, I think, are the symbols of the 'victorious will'. The ideas are high but they are worth striving for!

On the crucial day of 6 September 1965, when India had a distinct advantage over Pakistan because of the surprise element and superior tactic, Lieutenant Generals Harbakhsh Singh's Singh and J.S. Dhillon visited the front to assess the situation. The former describes the scene in his book. "We were directed by the Divisional Military Police to the General Officer Commanding, Maj. Gen. Niranjan Prasad, who was hiding in a recently irrigated sugarcane field! He came out to receive us, with his boots covered in wet mud. He had no head cover, nor was he wearing any badges of rank. He had stubble on his face, not having shaved, contrary to custom before the start of an operation. Seeing him in such a state, the first question I asked him was whether he was the General Officer commanding a Division or a coolie. Why had he removed his badges of rank and not shaved, I asked? Of course, he had no answer".

After he was given a second chance and again failed, he was removed from his command. Subsequently, when Radio Pakistan started reading out the incriminating contents of his personal diary which he had left in his abandoned official vehicle on the following day (September 7), the government asked him to resign.

It has been my practice, when in a position of command, to always give my subordinates due warning and another chance to mend their ways. During the war with Pakistan in 1965, when I found Major General Niranjan Prasad in a disoriented state, I decided to give him another chance. With this in view, I sent for the commander of his reserve brigade, Brigadier Pathak, and gave him orders, in the presence of Major General Niranjan Prasad and his Corps Commander, Lt Gen Dhillon, to recapture the ground lost by the leading brigade of the division, and made Major General Niranjan Prasad responsible to see that the orders were carried out. It was only after the latter failed to supervise the conduct of these orders that I agreed, on his Corps Commander's recommendation, to remove him from command of the division.

A similar case was that of Major General DB Chopra, an engineer officer, promoted to command 10 Infantry Division at Akhnoor, in Jammu and Kashmir. He had recommended, and asked for permission from his Corps Commander, Lt Gen Kashmir Katoch, to withdraw his Brigade at Jaurian, which was close to the enemy, during the night of 3/4 September. I had to countermand his advice as impracticable, and decided that I would myself arrive at Akhnoor, with the Corps Commander, at 9 a.m. on the morning of 4 September, and would give orders for the withdrawal of the Jaurian Brigade only after studying the situation for myself. Till then the brigade was ordered to stay where it was. I arrived at Akhnoor along with the Corps Commander, and learnt that so far all was well with the Jaurian Brigade. However, it appeared that the personnel of a field regiment, supporting the Jaurian Brigade, had deserted enmasse, leaving behind their guns, vehicles and stacked ammunition. I ordered the Divisional Commander, in the presence of his Corps Commander, to pass orders that afternoon for the withdrawal of the Jaurian Brigade that night, but only after all the guns, vehicles and ammunition left behind by the field regiment had been collected. Unfortunately he failed to do so, and it was on the recommendation of his Corps Commander that I had to order his removal. These were two cases of removal from command of senior officers. There were others of junior rank who were also found deficient in commanding their troops during the war and had to be removed from command, but only after due warning had been given.

CAREER

1 Oct 1913	Born	
1928	Matriculation, Ranbir High School	Sangrur
1929	Government College	Lahore
Mar 1933	Joined Indian Military Academy	Dehradun
Jul 1935	Commissioned in British Indian Army	
	2nd Bn Argyll and Sutherland Highlanders	Rawalpindi
Jul 1936	5th Bn/11th Sikh Regiment	Aurangabad
Sep 1938		Razmak
Apr 1939		Malaya
Jan 1940	Wounded in action	
	Prisoner of War	
Apr 1945	4th Bn Sikh Regiment (Second-in-Command)	
Feb 1947	Staff College Course	Quetta
Oct 1947	Deputy Commander, 161 Inf Bde	Kashmir
	Commander, Srinagar Garrison	
Dec 1947	Commanding Officer, 1 Sikh	
Apr 1948	Commander, 163 Infantry Brigade	
July 1949	Deputy Commandant, Indian Military Academy	Dehradun
Jan 1950	BGS, HQ Western Command	Shimla
Mar 1952	Appointed Colonel of the Sikh Regiment	
Sep 1956	Director of Infantry, Army HQ	New Delhi
Nov 1957	Imperial Defence College Course	London
Nov 1958	GOC 27 Infantry Division	Jalandhar
Nov 1959	GOC 5 Infantry Division	Jalandhar
Jul 1961	COS, HQ Western Command	Shimla
Oct 1962	GOC 4 Corps	Tezpur
Oct 1962	GOC 33 Corps	Siliguri
Nov 1964	GOC-in-C, HQ Western Command	Shimla
Sep 1969	Retirement	
Sep 1971	Relinquish Colonel of the Sikh Regiment	
14 Dec 1999	Died	New Delhi